DRAGON LIZARDS OF KOMODO

An Expedition to the Lost World of the Dutch East Indies

The wilderness of romantic Komodo.

DRAGON LIZARDS OF KOMODO

An Expedition to the Lost World of the Dutch East Indies

By

W. DOUGLAS BURDEN

APPROVED BY THE BOONE AND CROCKETT CLUB

With 52 Illustrations

B&C
CLASSICS
MISSOULA, MONTANA | 2021

Dragon Lizards of Komodo

By W. Douglas Burden

Originally published in 1927.
Reprinted in 2021 as part of
Boone and Crockett Club's series,
B&C Classics.

Paperback ISBN: 978-1-940860-41-1
ePub ISBN: 978-1-940860-42-8
Published November 2021

Published in the United States of America
by the
Boone and Crockett Club
250 Station Drive, Missoula, Montana 59801
Phone (406) 542-1888
Fax (406) 542-0784
Toll-Free (888) 840-4868 (book orders only)
www.boone-crockett.org

MESSAGE FROM THE PUBLISHER

THE Boone and Crockett Club was founded by Theodore Roosevelt and George Bird Grinnell in 1887. Two years earlier, Grinnell, then editor of *Forest and Stream,* wrote a critical review of Roosevelt's book, *Hunting Trips of a Ranchman.* Roosevelt paid him a visit to discuss the matter. During that meeting Grinnell presented a strong case about his concerns on the future of hunting and conservation. TR was in agreement, and thus began a lifelong friendship that led to the founding of the Boone and Crockett Club, the first private hunting and conservation organization in North America. The two also went on to collaborate on numerous books about hunting, conservation, exploration, and adventure. Since its early days, B&C has had a strong tie with publishing and furthering hunting and conservation.

In 2012, we launched our B&C Classics series of hunting and adventure books, including works from TR and Grinnell, as well as William T. Hornaday, Charles Sheldon, Frederick C. Selous and other adventurers from the late 1800s through the early 1900s. Each title in the B&C Classics series is selected by a committee of vintage hunting literature experts and is authored by a Boone and Crockett Club member.

Unlike other reprints of these hunting and adventure books, the B&C Classics series has been meticulously converted resulting in high-quality, digitally remastered eBooks and paperback editions. Many are complete with vintage photos and drawings not found in other editions. This attention to detail helps transport readers back to a time when hunting trips didn't happen over a weekend, but were adventures that spanned weeks, months, or even years.

We hope you enjoy the books we've selected for this series. They will give you a strong sense of our hunting heritage and provide hours of entertainment for anyone who loves adventure and the outdoors.

JULIE L. TRIPP
B&C Director of Publications
MISSOULA, MONTANA

TO MY COMPANION IN THE
ADVENTURE OF LIFE

FOREWORD

Many members of the Boone and Crockett Club are wanderers over the face of the earth. In their goings and comings they are likely to see, to hear, and to remember much that is interesting and that is worth recording for the benefit of those whose travels have led them in other directions. One of the objects of the Club is to further such exchanges of experience among its members. It wishes also to offer to a growing non-member public, anxious to learn of such things, the opportunity to read of the sport and the science of distant lands.

It is thus the purpose of the Boone and Crockett Club to encourage the publication of volumes dealing with hunting, exploration and scientific inquiry, but it formally approves only those which have passed under the eye of the editorial committee. The volumes so approved differ in character from those made up of contributions from members and published by the Club itself, each of which is designated as "The Book of the Boone and Crockett Club."

This volume, written by a member of the Boone and Crockett Club, is approved by the Club's editorial committee and is recommended by the Club, and will be found to possess a vivid interest for the general public.

George Bird Grinnell.

New York City,
July 5, 1927.

PREFACE

I'm sure many readers will pick up this book and ask why the Boone and Crockett Club would include a book about giant lizards in our B&C Classics Series. It's a good question with an intriguing answer!

I was first made aware of this title over 20 years ago when I was the managing editor of *Fair Chase* magazine. B&C Member Theodore J. Holsten contributed a great column wherein he highlighted long-time members and the books they had written. Holsten's Fall 1998 column was titled "Douglas Burden and His Search for the Wilderness." He wrote of Burden's adventures across the globe in the 1920s, including "stories that true dragons still exist on earth...". This piqued my curiosity, but my own quest for dragons would surface more than a decade later.

It wasn't until 2010 that I discovered the tie between Burden's dragon lizards, and two other B&C Members—Merian Cooper and Carl Akeley—and the one and only *King Kong*. I was doing research for descriptive signs to accompany several artifacts and books that we planned on displaying in our Visitor's Gallery. I discovered that Cooper was close friends with Burden and it's rumored that Burden's book was the inspiration for his 1933 movie, *King Kong*. The similarities are many—from adventurers exploring the Far East to the capture and exhibition of the "beast" in New York City. We also have on display the motion picture camera invented by Akeley, which was used to film the original *King Kong*.

Dragon Lizards of Komodo is a prime example of the adventurous spirit of many early B&C Members. They weren't just hunters, but explorers. We owe a lot to their discoveries and tales of far away lands and the animals they researched and collected.

Julie L. Tripp.

Missoula, Montana
October 13, 2021.

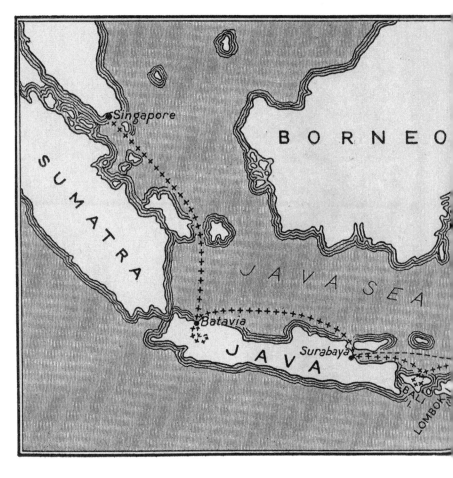

CONTENTS

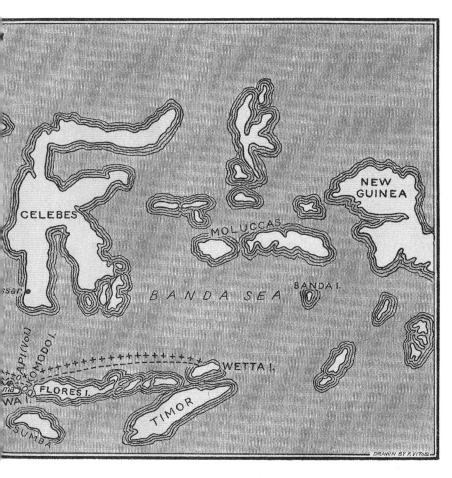

CELEBES

NEW
GUINEA

MOLUCCAS

BANDA I.

BANDA SEA

ssar

API(Vol)

KOMODO I.

WETTA I.

FLORES I.

WA I.

TIMOR

SUMBA

DRAWN BY F. VITOR

ILLUSTRATIONS

DRAGON LIZARDS OF KOMODO

An Expedition to the Lost World of
the Dutch East Indies

DRAGON LIZARDS OF KOMODO

CHAPTER I

INTRODUCTION

IF any man with sporting tastes and a real interest in natural history were told that true dragons were still living on a remote, little known island of the East Indies, what would he do? Allow me to answer the question.

First of all, he would try to make sure that the reports were founded on fact, and then, having satisfied himself, he would begin, a little secretly, perhaps, to lay his plans.

A man who has once lived in tropical jungles is a prey all his life, not only to recurring fevers, but to something perhaps more insidious; namely, a desire to return—a desire, I may say, that is difficult to deny. It was three years since I had been in the jungle—time enough to allow the imagination free rein.

So I came home one fine evening not long ago across Central Park and asked my wife how she would like to go dragon hunting. The idea fired her with enthusiasm; and, when I told her that these beasts were the very ones which had given rise to all the dragons of mythology and of the Chinese flag, she succumbed at once, and accordingly we began to concoct our plans.

First of all, I took the matter up with the authorities of the American Museum of Natural History, and such was the enthusiasm and backing of President Osborn and the Museum organization that from the start success seemed assured.

Then I wrote to Defosse, an old friend of mine, who has spent his life in the jungles of Indo China, whose skill at handling natives, and whose genius in the bush would make him of inestimable value. When this wonderful old hunter agreed to join us at Singapore, there was no longer any question of our being able to capture the animal alive. It would have been foolish, however, to limit ourself to a collection of dragons. Few scientists have been to the Lesser Sunda Islands, the group to which Komodo belongs, and, as there are many geological and zoogeographic problems in this region, our opportunities were exceptional.

The birds of the Lesser Sunda Islands are well known. So, also, are the mammals, but, since only a few collectors of reptiles and amphibians have investigated the region, we determined to make it a herpetological expedition. Dr. E. R. Dunn of Smith College, one of the leading herpetologists of this country, had been dreaming of Komodo for years, so that no persuasion was necessary when we suggested that he accompany us.

The next question concerned motion picture photography. A moving picture record of the largest lizards in the world would make an important and necessary contribution. It soon became evident that a first-class camera man, taken all the way from New York, involved an enormous and quite unnecessary expenditure. Accordingly, with the assistance of Mr. Park of Pathé News, arrangements were made to secure at small expense a Chinese camera man from Pathé Frères, Singapore.

As for still photography, Mrs. B. had been preparing herself for some time past for just such an opportunity, and, under the instructions of a delightful old photographer, Mr. Heim, was already exhibiting unusual skill.

So much for the personnel of the expedition.

The next question was, how were we to reach Komodo? An examination of some charts revealed an excellent harbor on the east coast of the island, but the sailing directions also spoke of sunken reefs and tidal currents which rendered navigation extremely hazardous. After a careful investigation of transportation facilities, it became evident that it would be essential to secure the cooperation of the Dutch Government. This very important phase of the preparation was taken up by the Hon. Richard Tobin, American Minister to The Hague, and the Hon. Joseph Grew, Under-Secretary of State. These two gentlemen took infinite pains and trouble in our behalf, and as a result of their diplomatic negotiations, the Dutch Government was kind enough to present us with a beautiful little four, hundred-ton steam yacht which carried us not only the seven hundred miles from Batavia to Komodo, but away on out to the Island of Wetar, which lies at the extreme eastern end of the Lesser Sunda chain.

I mentioned above that I had been somewhat secretive with regard to our plans, and yet, while Dr. Noble—curator of herpetology in the American Museum—and I were working over the details of equipment, vague rumors of rival expeditions kept coming to our ears. In spite of all the precaution we took, the reader will be interested to hear that after we left New York no less than three expeditions suddenly announced to the newspapers that they were setting out to capture the huge dragons of Komodo. I pictured all sorts of unpleasant episodes—Komodo is a small island. Three expeditions working there at the same time might have disastrous results. It was beginning to take on the aspects of a rush—not a gold rush, but a dragon rush.

Before concluding this introductory chapter, I feel that a few words about the dragon lizards themselves are necessary. I have been asked repeatedly if it is really true that these beasts are prehistoric—that favorite epithet of the newspapers, and, for the reason that the term is rather meaningless, I confess to finding the question difficult to answer. In the literal sense, every living organism is prehistoric, for are we not all, man included, the outcome of millions of years of evolution? If, however, the word has come to mean great age with little change, it is correctly applied to these carnivorous lizards of Komodo. For the truth is that they are the oldest of living lizards, dating as a genus back to early Eocene time, the beginning of the age of mammals. In other words, the ponderous reptiles that we watched and caught and killed among the volcanic pinnacles of an East Indian island are, with only a few specific differences, exactly the same as those that were crawling around over the face of this earth over sixty million years ago. It is interesting to note, however, that the species *komodoensis* is not the largest which the genus has evolved. There was one still greater which we know lived during the Stone Age of man, in northern Australia. This beast was thirty feet long and weighed, it has been estimated, over three thousand pounds. I was glad we did not find them disporting themselves on Komodo.

It may be well to mention briefly how these Komodo lizards happened to be discovered. Komodo, as I have already stated, is a very small island twenty-two miles long by twelve in width. Until recently, it was uninhabited, and as it is very difficult to reach, no naturalists, not even A. R. Wallace, the most famous traveller in this region, had set foot on the island. In 1912, some pearl fishermen anchored in a harbor there. These men substantiated native rumors of the dragons, with the result that P. A. Ouwens, of the Zoological Museum at Buitenzorg, Java, sent collectors to Komodo. When these men brought back a few specimens, Ouwens published the first description of the animal, which he called *Varanus komodoensis*. Then came the war, and the dragon lizards were temporarily forgotten.

Not long ago Dr. Noble told me about *Varanus komodoensis*, and the island of Komodo. Soon afterwards we were making our preparations for departure.

My wife and I sailed from San Francisco for China, where we expected to join Dr. Roy Chapman Andrews, and with him to go for a few days up into the Gobi Desert to see the wonderful work that the Central Asiatic Expedition was doing there. Dr. Dunn was sailing by way of the Indian Ocean. We parted company in New York and set out in opposite directions to meet on the other side of the world.

The Expedition was successful in its purpose of securing, dead and alive, a representative series of these antediluvian monsters. We brought home fourteen specimens, two living ones for the Bronx Zoo, and twelve dead animals for an exhibition group in the American Museum of Natural History.

Yet many interesting questions relative to *Varanus komodoensis* remain unanswered. In spite of a careful study of these lizards—or dragon lizards, as they are called, for they are the largest lizards in the world—we still have much to learn. We do not know, for example, what age they attain. Whether the two beasts that reached the zoo were ten years old or a hundred, we have not the slightest idea. Moreover, it is a curious fact that Komodo is geologically recent. Thus, we have a very ancient animal living on a young island: that is, an island that has recently risen above the level of the sea. How did he get there? Whence did he come? Why is he restricted to Komodo and a few small neighboring islands? What conditions have enabled him to survive in this isolated district? The journey to a distant land often entails unsought adventures and strange experiences. Travel in the Far East is always thrilling, but when the Far East is at war, the excitement is redoubled. With this brief introduction, let us turn, therefore, to the adventures that even made the outward trip to Java unusually fascinating.

CHAPTER II

IN THE DUST OF A CHINESE WAR

AFTER a long, rough passage across the Pacific, we reached Yokohama, took a hasty look at what little remains of that ruined city, and went on down the same night to Kyoto, the delightful pleasure city of Japan.

The question that interested us most of all was how to reach Peking. B. and I both had a mania to get there. The railroad communications with Shanghai were cut. Chang Tso-lin, with his Fungtien troops, blocked the Mukden route. The Japanese newspapers even stated that no trains were running between Tientsin and the capital, 80 miles away.

We soon had a cable from Roy Andrews, leader of the Third Asiatic Expedition of the American Museum of Natural History. It said: "Will meet you Tientsin and motor you up." That solved the problem temporarily, but two days later, the newspaper accounts gave us something to worry about. "Severe fighting between Peking and Tientsin." "Mukden Forces advancing on Capital; Peking in danger." "All communications cut, food scarce, bombs dropping every day." Moreover, a closer perusal revealed the distressing news that the Legations had renounced responsibility for foreigners travelling in China. It did not sound promising.

Of course I was not overanxious to take my wife into the thick of a fight. A few years ago a Chinese war was subject to ridicule. It wasn't war at all—just stage play, and foreigners amused themselves by photographing the battles, and joking about them. But almost overnight the character of the fighting changed. The Chinese had suddenly become serious, and that which such a short time ago was a mere game of chess, a complex series of moves and counter-moves, had taken on the aspects of an honest-to-God war.

I felt like abandoning the Peking project altogether, for we were still far enough from China to see the situation in perspective.

However, just to make sure that we weren't really missing a fine show, something that perhaps we would never forget, I cabled Roy again, asking if conditions still warranted our coming. The answer reached us in Kobe—just one word: "Come!"

I had expected as much, for I knew Andrews pretty well. I could easily understand how a man of his sporting instinct would consider it a crime to turn down such a glorious opportunity for adventure. Then, too, I knew the attitude of the foreigners in Peking; they are so accustomed to sitting on the edge of a smouldering volcano, as it were, that they rather like it. It acts as a tonic, and when the eruption takes place, as in the case of the Boxer rebellion, it catches them unawares.

However, I said to my wife, "There is plenty of time to be careful and to play safe when we're a doddering old couple, tottering on the edge of the grave. Let's go!"

So, with that, we jumped on a dirty Japanese freighter, the *Chosa Maru*, and sailed down the inland sea on our way to war-torn China. For the present, at least, Komodo and the dragon lizards were forgotten. Anticipation of excitement to come made us rather casual in our appreciation of the beauties of the inland sea, where multicolored sails are seen like birds banking against the blue. The south shore of Korea, (a remarkable coastline of submergence, with its islands and capes and drowned valleys) came up over the horizon, was enjoyed, and fell astern.

In five and a half days—the time it takes to cross the Atlantic Ocean—we found ourselves twisting and turning up a shallow, muddy river, towards Tientsin. And when the *Chosa Maru* docked at nine o'clock in the evening, there was no Roy Andrews to meet us.

On arriving at the hotel, we discovered the reason. The situation had become much more serious. The gates of Peking were closed and sand-bagged. All communications were cut. Severe fighting was going on near *Tungchow*, about twenty miles outside of the capital. Residents of Tientsin told us that no foreigners had gotten in or out of Peking for a week, and that there was no prospect of getting through for another ten days. Apparently, General Chang Tso-lin had chosen this particular time to stage his last drive on the capital, and in the face of the Mukden hordes, the Christian general, Feng Yu-hsiang, who had been holding Peking for many months, would be forced to evacuate. It was simply a question of time, but things move so slowly in China that this bit of information was far from encouraging. We were horribly depressed—so near our goal, and yet so far—marooned in a dull place like Tientsin!

Meantime, we could only wait and hope for the best. Of course, no tourists were travelling at the time, but there were many business men who were anxious to get through, and, what with everybody waiting at the hotel to hear the latest rumors and reports, the excitement ran high. Several men had made the attempt on horseback, but reappeared days later, having narrowly escaped with their lives. Anti-foreign feeling has increased tremendously in the last three years. Those who

Mrs. Andrews, Lou, Roy Chapman Andrews and Mrs. Burden enjoying afternoon tea at the Andrew compound

reside in China hardly seemed to be aware of a change that struck me very forcibly. It is noticeable everywhere that the foreigner is no longer a mere distrusted foreigner. He is a "foreign devil," with the emphasis on the word devil.

We had been in Tientsin only two days when, on our way to luncheon, B. and I were introduced to an American, McCann by name.

"I understand," he said, "that you want to get up to Peking. My wife is sick in the hospital there, and I am going to try to get through to her this afternoon. I have room for you, if you want to risk it, but you will have to be ready to leave in exactly half an hour."

We jumped at the opportunity, for we knew that this was our only chance to reach the gates before 6 P.M. McCann was a remarkable fellow who had been brought up in China. He spoke the Chinese dialects like a native, and he had such a complete knowledge of Chinese character that he could handle the people with the most amazing dexterity. In half an hour we were ready with one handbag apiece, and at 2 o'clock we leapt into the car, and were off at top speed, racing through the streets of Tientsin, with the horn tooting the entire time. The most nerve-racking automobile ride I ever hope to experience had begun. Aside from everything else, it was a race against time, with time a 10 to I favorite.

The early part of the trip has already been recorded by my wife.

"You see," she writes, "we were the first foreigners to start, so, as I discovered later on, no one expected to see us again. However, little realizing the danger, I rode blithely on, enjoying the scenery, and watching the lines of refugees that streamed by us on their way to Tientsin. When they cursed at us, I smiled sweetly, taking it as a greeting, and I thought it strange the sea of yellow faces looked back so sullenly through narrowed eyes. The country on either side of the wind-swept road was barren. China has frequently been described as a great grave-yard, and I remember noticing countless graves, or rather, mounds of earth, piled up pyramid fashion, and varying according to the dignity of the interred.

"The fields were practically deserted. The young, able-bodied men had been conscripted. A few decrepit starving old farmers were out plowing their fields. Men with ropes over their shoulders took the place of the oxen and horses stolen by the victorious army in their advance. There one had a picture of poor old battle-scarred China, and there was an example of the unflagging energy that makes China great. However crippled the Chinese dragon may be, his pulse always beats strong.

"Meantime, we sped on our way. All went well until some officers of Chang's rear guard stopped us. Later on, McCann told us that they had asked 'what the devil we thought we were doing,' and had cursed us roundly. It was nice of them to do this instead of the more customary proceeding in war territory of opening fire on us with no questions asked.

"However, after much talky-talk, in which it was evident that McCann displayed consummate skill, he suddenly turned to me and said, 'We haven't a chance without a pass. Have you any calling cards?' By the grace of God, I had, and they worked like magic. Without, of course, understanding a word of what was written on these insignificant looking documents, the soldiers pocketed them with a great show of 'face' and said, 'Pass!' How typical of the Chinese! The maneuver worked so famously that we used it four more times when we were held up, with rifles thrust into our faces and bayonets bristling around us. To think of my innocent little cards serving such a purpose 1 It was too funny. At any rate, we

miraculously kept going, over gun emplacements, and
through partly filled trenches, which we would hit at our
usual thirty-five miles per hour. Thirty five miles does not
sound like much, but on that road, so badly cut to pieces,
it was more punishment than I dreamed any car would
stand. I was in front, where it wasn't so bad, but Douglas,
who was in the back seat, had some bad cracks, and was
nearly thrown through the roof.

"On we dashed through groveling villages of mud huts,
and gangs of conscripted farmers, who, fortunately for
us, were working on the road to make it possible for
Chang to retreat, should he find the maneuver necessary.
Suddenly, we saw a broken down car ahead of us. A general
and a couple of subordinate officers were working over
it. We offered the general a lift, which he accepted. We
discovered, incidentally, that he was the head of Chang
Tso-lin's air force, and might well have been the very man
who had been dropping bombs on Peking, some of which,
no doubt, had nearly killed Roy Andrews. However, this
encounter later proved a life-saver for us, though it might
have meant just the reverse. If we had met any of his
enemies, we should all have been shot down like nine-pins.
McCann, having whispered to me that the general was our
best bet, was driving like a fiend.

"We had not gone far, however, when clouds of smoke
began coming up under my feet. We continued to try to
push on through a particularly bad piece of road before
stopping, when McCann suddenly threw on the brakes
and yelled, 'Jump!' He tore up the floor-boards and
tongues of flame shot up. He swept up armfuls of mud
and dirt from the road to throw on the flames, so we
all followed suit, and soon had the fire out. I remember
noting at this point that when our Chinese worthy offered
me a cigarette, his expression had not changed one whit.

16

A comfortable way to travel. The author's wife going up to one of the temples in the Western Hills.

"The fire was out, but it looked as though our wonderful ride had come to an end, and if we had not had the most expert mechanic and driver, we never would have succeeded in getting started again. Somehow he fixed it, and so we went on, driving more recklessly than ever, as the sun sank low in the heavens.

"Late in the evening, *Tungchow*, gray, old, and weary-looking, loomed out of the plain. That ancient sea-port of Peking has suffered countless wars and sieges and famines in her history, and as we jostled and bumped through the tottering gates, we ran suddenly into the tail-end of another devastating army. *Tungchow*, tired and breathless, seemed to be deserted. Fighting, looting and head-chopping had been her portion of the day's fare. Dirt from the heels of the advancing army sifted up over the shell-torn walls. It hung over the whole city like an ominous cloud. All day long the Mukden troops had been looting. In the morning they had entered a prosperous city: in the evening they vacated a barren wilderness of bricks. The American Mission school stood alone, a sanctuary untouched. We swept into the compound, and inside of a minute, a crowd of missionaries had gathered around us.

"They told us that no one had gotten in or out of Peking for days, and that, although it was only a matter of fifteen miles to the capital, the entire road was swarming with troops and that the situation at Peking was doubtless very serious. The general we had picked up could not possibly be of any use to us in getting into the city. We had all better jump right out and spend the next week or ten days with them. To tell the truth, they painted such a desperate picture that D. considered it foolhardy for me to proceed further."

When my wife had, at my special request, jumped out of the car, I was much relieved, for the troops had by this time left

Tungchow, and I knew that she was perfectly safe in the mission compound. As for myself, I could not bear to give up our dash on Peking, and determined to start on again immediately with McCann and the general—a decision hastily made, which later on I regretted, as it was my duty to remain with her.

However, McCann knew that rumor in China is worthless, for what is true one hour is not true the next, and, as the fortunes of war cannot be prophesied, we decided to risk it. Moreover, it seemed obvious that if we could get through the gates of Peking that night, it would be possible to come back for B. the next day.

The general himself had no idea whether we could get through. The missionaries had described fighting and looting outside the gates of Peking. If this was true, he might run into his enemies at any minute.

All this has taken a long time to explain, but actually, we flew into the compound and flew out again almost in the same breath. We had not a minute to lose. It was now twenty minutes past five, and the most romantic city in the world lay ahead of us, somewhere in the fling. McCann looked like Barney Oldfield himself. He seemed to be devouring the dusty road. The general sat beside me, twitching nervously. For a couple of miles we had a fairly clear road, and then we caught up with the main body of the advancing army, and immediately were in the thick of it. No one who has not travelled in a motor car through densely populated sections of China can picture the turmoil created by this detestable contrivance of the Western world. Horses, mules and donkeys, all unaccustomed to the sight of a motor car, are frightened out of their senses. They rear and plunge and break loose from their harness, while their unfortunate drivers risk their very lives in attempts to hold them in. They gallop off like wild things, jumping over embankments, and across ditches, leaving a twisted wreckage of smashed carts, broken wheels and supplies in their wake. Not infrequently, Chinese coolies are caught in the traces and run down by the clumsy, overloaded studded wheel carts. Small wonder that the foreigner is hated in China.

And, yet, we had to get through. And the only way a path could be cleared ahead of us was by tooting the horn. Then, always, pandemonium broke loose, and the Chinese officers and soldiers cursed us as long as we remained in sight. The troops were itching to take a crack at us. If they had done so, the Legation would not have been responsible, for we were travelling at our own risk. When we were forced to stop every now and then, a swarm of cruel yellow faces crowded around, leering at us. They spat, they cursed, they were fairly bursting with hatred. And, whenever they became too vehement, General Chow would put his head out and give a few sharp orders. If the slightest thing had gone wrong the last chapter of our story would have been told right there in the dust and dirt of the Peking-Tientsin road.

An automobile ride of this sort is pure torture, and yet, somehow, adventure is its own reward. Now that our headlights had been ruined by the fire, I began to wonder how we could hope to find our way back in the dark along the crowded road to *Tungchow*, if we should fail, as it was practically certain we would, to get through the gates. If we had to spend the night outside the walls of the city, amidst the swarms of looting soldiery—well I didn't like to think of it.

Just after sunset, the great walls, battlements and watch towers of the Chinese capital showed up black against the sky—a grim spectacle. Away beyond, I could see the lights and shadows of the western hills mellowed and softened in the purple distance. There was our objective, the massive eastern gate, itself a great fortress towering from the plain into a golden sky.

How many times had these formidable walls withstood

the advance of mighty armies, how many times had they si-
lenced the "rhythmic tread of thousands!" Once more the gates
were closed to an invader, and we, foolish children, proposed
to pass through the walls that held an entire army at bay. What
could we do against anything so impregnable?

Finally, as we dashed madly along the settlements that
have grown up outside the walls, dusk fell upon the plain. Here
were gun carriages and thousands of carts carrying provisions
for the army all jumbled up together. Here were a fierce-look-
ing group of mounted Cossacks, who had joined the Chinese
troops for want of a mouthful to eat. Here was an execution
ground, with crowds of soldiers milling around. Mean-looking
they were, with bestial expressions. All day long they had been
lopping off heads wherever they met with resistance—a cus-
tom as old as China herself. One of these heads, quite fresh,
hung by the roadside. The executioners were on the job, night
and day. We tried to find out why, but nobody knew, except
that the Fungtien troops wanted some heads to adorn the gates
of the city, as a grewsome witness to their victorious advance.

At last, with a final burst of reckless driving, we drew
up under the very shadow of the great eastern gate. Swarms of
soldiers blocked our way. Our general ordered them aside and
stepped briskly up to where two gigantic studded doors stood
closed, bolted and sandbagged. McCann and I held our breath.
Now that our car had stopped, we could hear the shouts and
cries of the rabble, the curses of the soldiery, and the sound
of gongs and drums that rose all together in one great hum
into the night. The general was talking now. Someone had
moved a sliding panel from within. Presently he fumbled with
some papers and shoved them through. Then, after another
minute, he quietly resumed his seat in the car. "It is all right,"
he murmured in Chinese. "They are opening the gates. I was
expected. I am to be in charge of Peking."

Imagine my feelings, when McCann translated these words! What luck! We had picked up, quite by chance, about the only man in all China who could have had the gates opened.

After waiting about ten minutes, during which the sandbags were being removed, there was a loud jangling of bolts and chains, and with heavy creakings the ponderous doors swung open before us. The next second the gates closed, and we were safe within the walls of Peking. How I cursed myself for having made B. get out at *Tungchow*! As the general had been expected, crowds lined the streets to witness his magnificent entry. Suddenly, I heard somebody screaming my name, and there, to my great astonishment, was Roy Andrews stepping out of the crowd to greet me. He was, if anything, more surprised than I was, for, as he had not received our wire from Tientsin, he did not even know that we were in China. For two days both he and the French minister had been trying in vain to have the gates opened. Every pretext had been used, and nothing was of any avail. Then, as he wrote later,

> "Just as the police in charge of the gates had reiterated that they were under strict orders not to open them, they suddenly added, 'but please draw your car to one side for a moment, because a very important general is about to arrive.' And, just as I backed my car out of the way, the gates swung open, and, amid the acclamations of the multitude, in came Douglas. It was a triumphal entry, if there ever was one, and seemed miraculous."

A few moments later I was wining and dining in one of the most luxurious compounds of Peking, the temple of an old Manchu princess, now the headquarters of the Third Asiatic Expedition, owned by Roy Andrews. The estimable Low was waiting upon me, silent-footed, efficient and pleased. Under the circumstances, I could not help but think of poor B. When

22

Headquarters of the Third Asiatic Expedition, Peking.

I told Roy that I had left her at *Tungchow*, he looked positively frightened, but, of course, as might be expected, they thought in Peking that *Tungchow* was being swept off the map, whereas in *Tungchow*, the missionaries were certain that dreadful things were happening to Peking. But that is China all over. Nobody ever knows, and the rumors are always bad. Let us see therefore what kind of a time B. was really having.

"To go back to my pathetic side of it," she writes, "the minute the car dashed off, I realized, too late, that I had been hypnotized by all those sad-eyed missionaries, and had gotten out of the car when it was the very last thing I wanted to do. They had looked at me and shaken their heads, as much as to say, 'Don't take that poor young thing into the very jaws of death,' and the combination of their wills was overpowering. When the realization came over me that I was left alone in that God-forsaken spot, while the rest went on, I almost started running wildly after them. It made me absolutely frantic, and, of course, I was worried to death all the time that they were being shot at or massacred. Heaven knows how I lived through that night. There was nothing to do, however, but make the best of it, so off I went with a kind old missionary called Mrs. Stell. I cannot even attempt to describe her and the house in which she lived: no stage mission could be more exaggerated. Her mother, who had been in China 58 years in the same house, lived with her, and a picture of her father, the first missionary of *Tungchow*, hung over the mantel. Every other picture was biblical.

"After an hour or so, I was given a basin of hot water, and we adjourned to supper. When a prolonged grace had been said, I tried to eat something, but finally gave up, and retired early to bed in hopes of passing the time in oblivion. My state of mind, however, precluded sleep.

Of course, the firing on *Tungchow* had ceased, but the
bullet holes were everywhere, and no one knew what
might happen next. The Chinese were terrified and had
packed in solid in the cellars of the five foreign houses.,
A confused murmur arose from them all through that
terrible night. A doctor who had been at dinner told the
most dreadful tales of such numbers of wounded pouring
into the hospital that there was no place to put them,
nor food where with to feed them. Half the time, they
were just left to die. My kind hostess tried to reconcile me
to a two weeks' stay, as they all firmly believed that my
husband would be killed and that I should never reach
Peking. Already they treated me gently, as one bereaved,
or crazed, as no doubt I seemed to be. Nothing has ever
affected me in such a way, and I tossed in vain fury from
dark until a darker dawn. Of course I knew that, rather
than be marooned in that ghastly place, I should either
attempt to walk or ride to Peking. Anything would be
better than this dreadful inactivity. Desultory supply
trains were still passing by the gates all the time, so I crept
down to see what the possibility might be of getting a ride.
I was desperate, but the chances looked too slim, even to
me. I therefore returned for breakfast, and, once more,
hurt poor Mrs. Stell's feelings by being unable to choke
down a morsel of her especially pre pared food. She had
never seen any one from New York before, and treated
me as a rather break able curiosity. When I sat down, she
hardly knew where to look, as her own modest garments
swept voluminously up from the floor to a well-boned
collar pressing viciously into her chin.

"After breakfast we toddled around arm in arm, the aged
mother and I, she pathetically proud of her life's work in
those barren mission grounds. We entered some of the
crowded cellars, and it was a tragic sight—women and
children hopelessly huddled one on top of another day

and night, while their husbands foraged vainly for enough
food to fill their empty mouths. Most of these people had
nothing left them but the rags on their backs, and yet they
sat numbly accepting what fate offered, only now and
then attempting to still the incessant wails of their hungry
children. After this, I returned and tried to get Peking on
the telephone, but, of course, failed.

"About ten o'clock, Captain Armstrong turned up—an
American army officer who had been sent from Peking
some weeks before to help protect the mission in case it
were attacked. He suggested tennis to pass the time, but as
it was Sunday, this was forbidden. Then he suggested cards,
but as this also was forbidden, we ended by climbing the
church tower. From here, with a pair of field glasses, we
could see for miles around, and I watched with desperation
for some kind of car along the curving ribbon of white
road that stretched away into the west. All that could be
seen were crawling lines of dust-colored soldiers and carts,
and, far away, the black gates of Peking itself.

"I felt like Bluebeard's wife, calling to sister Anne. Hour
after hour dragged by, until my eyes were blurred with
watching. Then came a spark of hope. What was that black
object coming toward us, breaking through the waving
lines of soldiery? I was already running down the winding
stairway, when Armstrong's cry arrested me, 'Only a Red
Cross cart full of wounded.' Once more I returned to the
mission, and sat through another interminable meal. Then
back to my watch tower. Once more I descried a distant
speck on the horizon. Nearer it came and nearer, and still I
dared not hope. The minutes were endless. It was a car, but
was it the right one, and would it stop before the mission
gate? It did!

"My relief was too great; I could hardly face them. Yet, so
quickly does one recover from baseless worries that when I

*A Chinese vender on the streets of Peking. He goes gaily along
hurling his musical cries over the roof tops.*

did join them, it was as casually as though I had left them five minutes before at a garden party.

"Thus, after a grateful farewell to my good hostess, I fell into the car with Roy, Douglas and McCann, and started over the hellish bit of road between *Tungchow* and the city of our dreams."

It had proved rather simple to get through the gates to come to her rescue. Roy and McCann and I called on General Chow the morning after my arrival. Knowing that a Chinaman never forgets a debt, we put it up to the general that as we had helped him, it was his turn now to do us a favor. Accordingly, after the weather had been discussed, and all ceremonies observed á la Chinois, we obtained passes stating that we were advisors to the Chinese air force, going to *Tungchow* on business. But even with these papers in hand, it was a problem to get through the maze of soldiers that swarmed about the gates. Soldiers cannot read, so that passes are of precious little value in China. The men closed in on us from all sides so that we could not move. One burly, ape-like executioner, with low-hanging jaw and savage eyes that glowed dully, as if his joy in life were to sever heads, thrust his face within a foot of McCann's and cursed him. McCann smiled sweetly back, and then, making some tactful remark in Chinese about double handed execution swords—what magnificent instruments they are, and what a useful purpose they serve—he reached out and took hold of the hideous weapon. The ape-man, though an executioner by profession, and a bully by nature, was so dumbfounded by this amazing display of impudence that he released the weapon entirely. McCann passed the thing back to us. While Roy and I were examining the gory device, still hot from use, he continued to converse, with the result that, after the jingling of coins had been heard, our would-be assailant was out ahead, clearing the road for us. The man who, a moment before, was ready to run us through, had now come to our rescue. So much for a little tact and diplomacy in China. However, it would hardly be advisable for you or me to attempt to imitate McCann.

We had been caught in the same place for more than half an hour, but now we began to move ahead, forcing our way slowly, bit by bit, until at last we were clear on the open road, with only a few supply trains to bother us.

Roy showed us the place where, ten days before, soldiers had opened fired upon him. For more than one mile he was forced to run the gauntlet with the Chinese shooting out of the windows and doors of mud huts on either side of the road, and it was only their miserable marksmanship that saved him.

At about three o'clock we picked up B., and, after another nerve-racking ride back to Peking, the most noticeable feature of which was a fresh head hanging by the ear to a telegraph pole—probably the work of our friend the executioner—the relief on getting her finally safe and sound in the city was something to be remembered.

The war was now being waged to the northward, in the neighborhood of Hangkow pass. The Third Asiatic Expedition, therefore, could not get up to Kalgan, as they were blocked by the fighting, and all our brilliant plans fell through. Thus for two weeks B. and I gave ourselves up to the enjoyment of Peking.

Peking is a strange city. The attitude of the foreigners might almost be called an esprit de corps. When the airplanes were bombing the city, the foreigners amused themselves by attending bombing breakfasts at the Peking Hotel, where they could sit on the roof and watch the planes in their daily round of destruction. When Peking was falling, the foreigners were playing polo, dancing at the club, and enjoying a never-ending round of festivities. The more acute the situation becomes, the more Peking laughs, and the harder it plays. We were caught up by this spirit, and plunged at once into a perfect whirl of gayeties. Sometimes we lunched at beautiful temples tucked away in groves of verdure in the western hills, sometimes on a marble boat on the lake in the summer palace. The boat, the lake, the magnificent palace, all were built by that illustrious being the Empress Dowager and (here is the point) they were built with money raised particularly for a Chinese fleet. Thus do Orientals turn authority to their personal advantage. Once we went out some distance, to the Black Dragon Pool, a beautiful temple hidden in the hills. It was built by the last emperor for his concubines. The central pool, a deep body of spring-fed crystal water, is surrounded by galleries from which the Son of Heaven could watch his favorites disporting themselves. The bottom and sides were painted a velvet black, so that the delicate, ivory-colored bodies would shine more seductively by contrast. What a sensitive appreciation—what a magnificent touch of oriental ingenuity! Picture for a moment, the Black Dragon Pool, the languorous concubines, the wistaria that hangs like a canopy over the whole enclosure, and then, peering down into the water, the great autocrat himself, the monarch of the Chinese Empire!

Our servants followed us with tea, as they do everywhere one goes. It was always interesting the way Low, the Number One boy of the Andrews compound, would bow us out as we left, and then reappear ahead of us at any well-nigh inaccessible spot, ready to serve the most delicious lunch or tea at a moment's notice. Perhaps more amazing, however, was the fact that, on going out to dinner, we never had to tell our rickshaw boys where we were going. They always knew beforehand. One soon gets accustomed to these little sleight of hands. It is all part of the magic touch of the East. A friend of mine was even

Mrs. Burden on her way to breakfast.

more struck by this hidden force. Number One boy of the Peking Hotel had been instructed to see that this gentleman be presented with a small jade stamp on the morning of the third day after he left Peking. No information was given as to when he was leaving or where he was going. Several weeks later, the morning of the third day after his departure found him somewhere out in the middle of the Yellow Sea. On entering his cabin, he saw a small jade stamp placed in a conspicuous spot. He never discovered who had brought it there, but he was satisfied thenceforth as to the power and efficiency of the Chinese intelligence system.

Meantime, as the days flew by, we would stroll now and then over carpets of wood violets up to the Temple of Heaven, where the glorious blues and imperial yellow rival the colors of a sunset, or we would spend an afternoon at the jade pagoda or wander around the glowering walls of the Forbidden City; or else we would ease along in our rickshaws through the narrow, dirty, but fascinating streets, hunting some rare treasure of antiquity. And, between times always there was polo, and snipe-shooting and tennis and the dances, from which we would come home quietly through the dark streets in our rickshaws—those blissful inventions—listening to the soft patter of running feet, and the distant cries and songs of the Chinese that floated up into the starlight.

One night there was a dinner of a hundred courses, in the old Chinese style, served in the Winter Palace, and cooked, I must add, by the Emperor's cook, and served by his servants. No foreigner had ever been allowed there before. The dinner, as may well be imagined, was a rather painful affair, lasting for more than three hours, and consisting of shark's fins, and bird's nests, and fish lips, and duck's tongues, and all such appetizing morsels. When it was all over, we stepped upon the great canopied barges strung with lanterns, and were poled around the lake in the brilliant moonlight, until the cool fresh air had overcome the nauseating effects of the dinner.

But the most memorable feature of the Peking visit was the old Manchu temple in which we lived.

Imagine a compound of high walls, "enfolding sunny spots of greenery. "Imagine splashes of light that fill the court-yards, moon doorways that lead to secluded nooks where the song-birds sing, vistas of hanging verdure, and clumps of flowers that fill the air with their fragrance.

All Peking knew that we were shopping, with the result that early in the morning B. would come out of her room blinking, not from the brilliant light, but from the dazzling spectacle that greeted her eye; for the inner court was filled with the treasures of Cathay:— rich furs, amber figures, ivory, crystal and rare jade, amethyst, and blanc de chine that shone like the full moon She would fairly wade around amidst silks and brocades and damasks, while I examined one ancient blue glass bowl, or diminutive figure of antiquity delicate in color and design. And while we were revelling among these precious fabrics and carvings of the East, B. almost in a state of collapse at the extent of our purchases, the Chinese servants, silent and sure, were preparing breakfast. But now and again we could hear the weird calls and the hum of Chinese life that came out of the distance to remind us that the machine guns mounted on the roof of the temple were not placed there as mere decorations.

For, just outside of that entrancing courtyard, is the squalor of China. It is like living on a peaceful island in the midst of a restless Yellow Sea, and occasionally some unfortunate victim—perhaps guilty, perhaps not—was led past by the executioners to have his head chopped off.

CHAPTER III

DREAMY VAPORS
OF THE TROPICS

BEFORE leaving Peking, I found "Chu," our most priceless possession throughout our eastern travels. Some time ago, Chu had been my "boy," or bearer, as they say in India. I took him to Mongolia, the Philippines, and into the jungles of Indo-China, where his services as cook, in spite of frequent attacks of malarial fever, were marvellous. When this faithful boy volunteered to join us, I breathed a sigh of relief. He was a treasure, the type of servant one finds only in China. His wages were only ten dollars a month, and for that paltry sum there was nothing he wouldn't or couldn't do.

From then on, we travelled de luxe, and never worried our heads over anything. Our clothes were washed, sewed, pressed and laid out: our baths run, our bags packed and unpacked, our money scrupulously taken care of, and every smallest article was so carefully stowed away that Chu could put his hands on it at a moment's notice. And, meantime, as our baggage swelled from five to fourteen pieces, it appeared magically and followed us from place to place while we went ahead without a thought. For a few pennies a day Chu would find himself food and shelter, do all the work and keep us amused

The S. S. Dog on which we travelled more than 1500 miles. She is here seen putting in her last supplies before leaving Souraboya.

with stories in the most unbelievable pidgin English. He was one of the few servants who stuck to the Legation all through the Boxer rebellion.

And so, as we motored back over the same old road to Tientsin, we carried with us the first addition to our expedition. Tientsin I have already described as a ghastly place. The adjective may be too strong. Tientsin, along with Shanghai and Hongkong, are typical examples of Europe in the Orient, and for this reason I find them colorless, nondescript. They are seaports—the name covers a multitude of sins. But enough said: Tientsin, to my mind, is not worthy of further attention.

One black night early in May, we said goodbye to Roy and boarded the S.S. *Tungchow*, bound for Shanghai, a three days' run. On her last voyage, the *Tungchow* had been captured by Chinese pirates. The officers were killed and the first-class passengers looted. Then the pirates sailed their newly acquired yacht to South China, and put ashore at a small town near Swatow. These piracies are of frequent occurrence, especially as the culprits rarely fail to make a clean get-away. But how is it done? I had wondered myself how a big steamship could be captured by pirates—thinking, of course, that they boarded her from those small, picturesque sailing junks so familiar in pictures. But that isn't the way at all. It is very simple. They take passage in the steerage, and, although they are examined, it is a simple matter for them to smuggle arms on board. Then, when a ship is at sea, at a given signal they rush the bridge and kill the officers. The rest is easy.

About half way across the Yellow Sea a dense fog rolled down upon us, and for the rest of the trip we were immersed in it. The fog horn tooted monotonously, the great sickening rollers swept by as we crept foot by foot through that colorless, oily ocean. Occasionally shouts and screams from the steerage reminded us of a danger that we should otherwise have forgotten, or else, silence would fall ominously upon that quarter, so that we could picture a group of armed bandits preparing to rush the bridge. Not a pleasant prospect, to be at the mercy of a wild swarm of swarthy Chinese who value your life even less than they do their own. Aside from this, the trip was monotonous, and the passengers dull. It was a great relief, therefore, to put ashore at Shanghai, and go tearing up the Bund in a rickshaw, with those strapping coolies laughing and squabbling together as they ran.

Hardly were we comfortably ensconced in the Astor House, before a perfect stream of Chinese vendors of silks and furs and *objets d'art* began to arrive. A tailor proposed to make me silk shirts and underclothes and pongee suits and wrappers for the tropics. The price of a suit of highest quality of pongee made to order was eighteen dollars. The temptation was too great and I succumbed. But when I told him that I was sailing the following morning at 6 o'clock, and that it would therefore be impossible to do all the work in the allotted time, he astonished me not a little by replying, "easy can do." I therefore placed a large order, assuring him that I would not pay one cent if the clothes did not fit properly. He took the necessary measurements and went his way. At half past five the following morning, just half an hour before the *President Polk* weighed anchor, my tailor knocked at the cabin door. The shirts, the wrappers, the pongee suits, the underwear, all were perfect, and thus attired, I looked like a Palm Beach advertisement. In less than twenty hours my order had been filled. In New York it would have taken a month; moreover, a single pongee suit would have cost over a hundred dollars, and even then it probably would not fit. In the same length of time B. had some beautiful dresses made, and was as pleased with her purchases as I was with mine.

In a few hours we were steaming down the China coast,

enjoying the calm weather of the horse latitudes. Fortunately for us, the typhoon season had not begun. I say fortunately, because the China Sea is perhaps the worst place in the world for typhoons. These monstrous creations of nature usually form somewhere east of the Philippines. This region is their birthplace. Then, as fully developed demons of destruction they sweep westward over the islands, and swing north in the neighborhood of Hongkong, taking their toll of life as they go, till eventually they blow themselves out somewhere up near Japan. Two boats that I sailed on in these waters have since gone down with all hands. The S.S. *Loongsang*, a famous old hulk in oriental ports, was torn from her moorings in Hongkong harbor, smashed against the rocks and sunk. As the wind was blowing at 140 knots, any attempt at rescue was impossible. At the topmost pinnacle of the island of Hongkong, which can be seen for miles around, there is a meteorological observatory, and when the storm signals go up, thousands of Chinese fishing smacks that have wandered far out to sea turn and scurry for shelter.

We spent only a few hours at Hongkong. Manila is our next stop. A glassy sea stretches to the horizon, and the "round-the-world" passengers, an ignorant array of middle-class shop-keepers, pass the time gossiping and seeing the world. "Oh, look!" says one, sighting a thunder cloud that rolls up out of the west, "there comes a monsoon!" I was half sorry the northeast monsoon wasn't snorting down between Formosa and Luzon. That staunch scion of the U.S.A., with his tight-fitting trousers and his nasal twang would have received a liberal education.

As we approached Manila, it became hot, sultry, oppressive, damp. We were in the tropics at last. On landing we drove down the streets of the old Spanish city, sped past the Army and Navy Club, along the edge of Manila Bay, and through the grounds of Malacanyan, the palace of the Governor-general of

38

The Loongsang lurching into the Northeast monsoon. This famous old bulk has since gone down with all hands in a typhoon in Hongkong harbor.

the Philippine Islands. General Wood was away at Baguio, the summer capital, but I could remember well his magnificent bearing as he would stroll out to the porch for after -dinner coffee—a marvellous combination of towering strength and philosophical calm. There, comfortably ensconced behind a large cigar, he would tell us fascinating details of the Moro campaign and his early days in the Islands, while General McCoy and Colonel Johnson flavored the story with personal touches. And, while the General would sit thus, the serenity of a Buddha chiselled on his military features, the leader of the Philippine Senate, and other rank *mestizo* politicians were haggling and shouting vulgarly about a Philippine independence which the true Filipinos don't want, and ignorant, yapping Congressmen from the U.S.A., mere publicity seekers, would join the fray, adding their noisy clamor to that of their *mestizo* brothers.

We spent the day trying to keep cool, but failed hopelessly. At five P.M. we headed for Paxanyan, a place of deep pools and precipitous gorges, where lizards scuttle along the cliffs on either side. But we never reached it. Instead, we were forced to pass the night at an unkempt inn, where the air hung limp and breathless. One oil lamp flickered oppressively in the gloom. Everything dripped of humidity. A shuffling native woman thrust an unappetizing dinner before us. The flies buzzed. A white husband and half breed children eyed us silently from a corner. A balcony over the street supported our cots for the night, while the mosquito nets successfully trapped all the pests of the village and the natives crooned unceasingly below. The next morning we returned to Manila, our dispositions shattered, our clothes ruined, and our faces swollen with insect bites. So passed the lowest point on our journey around the world.

The trip to Singapore was a matter of five more days. The ship captain on that part of the trip deserves mention, as a

The gorge at Paxanyan where lizards scuttle along the cliffs on either side.

self-righteous old fanatic. To enumerate all the petty annoyances instigated by that worthy, which almost worked the passengers up to a point of open rebellion, would cover too many pages. The old toad was so afraid that there might be some illicit intrigues on board that he appointed himself special guardian of our morals.

B. and I took our cots up onto the top deck one hot night. We were severely reprimanded. Thereafter, no passengers were allowed on the top deck after 6 P.M. The next day, he saw a boy ducking a girl in the swimming pool. Thenceforth, men and women were not allowed to swim together—mornings for men, and afternoons for women. Small wonder that indignation among the passengers ran high. What if there were intrigues on board! At least, it would have given the bored passengers something to talk about. And, besides, who ever heard of a captain's meddling with the private affairs of passengers? Probably he was jealous. At all events, accustomed and well-fitted as he was to some old water-logged tramp, he certainly did not belong on the *Polk*. B. said she could have pricked his oily carcass.

In Singapore, the great melting pot of the East, we found Defosse waiting for us, and looking very sorry for himself in civilized surroundings. Except for an occasional visit to Saigon, he had not left his jungle for twenty-four years. I had lived with Defosse for over two months in the hunting country of Indo-China, and had acquired such respect for this extraordinary man that I want to introduce him to you here. To begin with his character is irreproachable. Courageous, scrupulously honest and truthful, a trained observer, a phenomenal shot, he gives no superficial evidence of his qualities.

To see him shuffling indolently down the streets of Singapore, with downcast countenance, one would never for a moment suspect that he was capable of great things—a hero in his own country. He is the type of man with whom one must live alone, to get to know him, whom one must see in action to understand. Always interested, he makes himself interesting by filling in the gaps of other people's memory with his own wide range of knowledge. A large part of his discourse concerns the elephant, the tiger, the buffalo, the sladang, and all the other wild animals whose intimate life-histories he has come to know so well. But he spices his anecdotes now and then with humorous bits concerning love and marriage among the jungle people; for, although moral himself, he holds no brief for morality, and, like all frontiersmen, he feels that a little flavoring goes a long way towards enlivening discourse.

The fact that Defosse is covered with scars from encounters with wild beasts of the jungle gives him a certain romantic interest. But he has the brains to sustain interest: he is a brilliant linguist, and, although a Frenchman, he has written for that arbiter of good English, the *Atlantic Monthly*. But, as too much eulogy without criticism becomes irksome, it is necessary to add that Defosse suffers one disadvantage from the free life he has led. He is too self-willed and independent to accommodate himself to a new environment. He thinks always in terms of Indo-China, and his perspective is, therefore, necessarily narrow.

Well, here he was, this really delightful old character, suffering agonies in the strange surroundings of Singapore, and out of his element with crowds of people. He was frightened to death of sea-sickness, and he insisted upon wearing his hunting outfit, for, as he said, "They are men's clothes." Always his thoughts went back to his family in the jungle—his native wife and his children, particularly the only one of his sons who has not died of malaria, and who is a chip of the old block.

From Pathé Frères, I secured the services of Lee Fai—a Chinese moving picture man who had been learning for two years how to take movies. Lee Fai was no ball of fire. He knew how to focus, set the stops and turn a crank, but beyond whatever ingenuity was necessary to perform such feats of mechanical skill his imagination did not stray. Lee Fai was delicate, frail and clumsy. He loved his siesta and hated to expend physical energy. But he was good-natured, cheerful and quiet—qualities which, on an expedition, are beyond estimation. Lee Fai never would or could talk you to death. Chu and he got along famously. Their conversations were a conglomeration of gesticulation, Mandarin Chinese, Malay and pidgin English, the result being enough to make any observer hilarious.

We were a weird outfit, as we left the Raffles Hotel and boarded the great Dutch liner for a two days' trip to Batavia.

That oceanic hotel was a revelation of efficiency after our Dollar liners, but the people were atrociously fat and self-satisfied and not a word of English was spoken. We spent most of our time studying Malay, the language of the East Indies, while the Dutch shovelled away their food all day long.

The sky was overcast, the air moist, for we were in the Doldrums, and the sultry, hot inflowing Trades spasmodically released a superabundance of water vapor. There were calms, great glassy patches of water, and storms and light breezes in alternating succession.

At Batavia, Dr. Dunn, who had already been in Java for two weeks, met us at the dock. He had two bomb shells to hurl at us. In the first place, he said that no boat could be obtained to go to Komodo, and in the second, that Komodo had been made into a preserve, and that hunting, therefore, was prohibited. This news fairly took my breath away. After travelling fifteen thousand miles to be told that my errand was fruitless!

However, there are bound to be reverses on every expedition, and I felt sure that something could be done. First of all, we installed ourselves in a hotel in Buitenzorg. Then I set out to carry my plea to officialdom. The Governor-general, having recently married, was up in the mountains at Tjipanas, so I wired for an audience with his Excellency. While waiting for an answer, we lost ourselves in admiration of Dutch fat and the ways of the white man in the tropics. As soon as the Dutch reach Java, they give in to the debilitating climate, the somnolent atmosphere of the East Indies. Then having assumed the national dress of pyjamas, they spend their time eating and sleeping. The combination of fat and pyjamas is unbelievable. The Dutch display none of the character and self-discipline of the British in India, and yet they are better off than the opium-smoking French of Saigon.

You see them at half past five, after a long siesta, still drugged with food and drink, and perspiring from every roll of fat, with their feet up on the veranda, husband and wife, big feet and little, down the line. There they sit during tea, sluggish even while eating, as though every ounce of energy had been drained from their bodies, almost too lazy to breathe, and unutterably bored, bored with existence, bored with themselves, bored with everything except, perhaps, eating and love-making. For they are a voluptuous people, these Dutch, who sit around endlessly inhaling the fumes of gin and bitters and the dreamy vapors of languorous tropic nights.

There is no caste system, no color line, in the East Indies. There seems at first sight to be a complete disintegration, a complete breaking down of social standards, such as we know them. And where is this getting the world, this intermarriage between race and race, this breaking down of the barriers of race consciousness? In the long run, as intermarriage becomes more and more frequent, does it not lead inevitably to one grand hodgepodge, one loathsome mixture of all races into a pigsty breed? An unattractive thought, perhaps, but sure of fulfillment, as long as racial intermarriage continues.

And yet, what right have I to speak thus deprecatingly of the Dutch, while the American tourist, that plague of the Orient, is at large? Only recently I read of certain acts of vandalism committed by Americans at the beautiful temples of Borobudur, Central Java, in their insatiable lust for souvenirs.

Furthermore, my attack on the slovenly habits of the Dutch is purely superficial. Behind their unattractive exterior, beneath the flesh, as it were, lies a great organization, and there are great men who have given their lives to Java, men of breeding, taste and judgment; men who have inherited the high qualities of statesmanship and the ability to govern. These men belong to the official class; it is they who have made Java. A certain measure of their work may be seen in the amazing increase in population (from 3,800,000 to over 40,000,000 in less than a hundred years). What a sign of prosperity! And yet, when all is said and done, what good is this increase in mere numbers? To what end this cluttering up the world with too many mouths?

Up to the present time, Java has been able to cope with this—shall I say—appalling increase. Her numerous volcanoes, at once a menace to life and property, have alone made this possible, for lava flows, when properly weathered, afford the richest soil. Java, therefore, is one luxuriant mass of verdure, and as the population is fairly evenly disseminated throughout the length and breadth of the land, instead of being all piled up in heaps, as it is in the western word, one would never guess that this beautiful island is one of the most thickly populated sections of the earth.

As for ourselves, the siesta hour was far from enjoyable. To begin with, the rooms are open, like verandas, with swinging doors, so that every body can look right in. We slept under nets, of course, on beds hard as boards, in order to be cool. There was not even a sheet to put over one, just a long bolster, called a "Dutch wife," to throw one's legs over, for comfort and coolness. Poor B. could not sleep. She simply groaned and tossed through the long hot afternoon, drowsy and logy from the effects of a glass of beer, but unable to induce the luxury of glorious oblivion.

In Buitenzorg, while still waiting for an audience with the Governor-general, B. and Defosse started off for a circus in a small, two-wheeled cart. When they climbed in at the back end, their combined weight fairly hoisted the unfortunate animal by his belly band into the air, so that he started off bouncing over the ground like a toy balloon.

Meanwhile, Dunn and I went "frogging." As we strolled through the Botanical Gardens in the evening, two little Malay girls, attired in their one piece sarongs, scampered up to us, smiling guiltily as they came. They saw that I carried a camera, and with a few words and many signs, soon made it quite evident that for a slight token they were desirous of posing in the nude. In fact, they could hardly wait to divest themselves of their garments. Doubtless, their naughtiness was at the instigation of their parents, so, while these dusky maidens sported like two immature Eves in the bed of a rocky stream, I took a few snapshots.

Pretty soon, the frogs were croaking in every direction, and the fire-flies, millions of them, playing around among the great black tree-trunks. The cool air of the evening, scented heavily with flowers of the jungle, brought back a rush of memories. Here was the atmosphere of Java, something that creeps into the blood, something insidious that can undermine constitution and character. You feel it as the blood becomes thinner and flows more freely through your veins.

Then the moon rose; first like a glowing coal, it shone dully through the rustling leaves, but as it sailed up over distant volcanoes, it emerged gradually, a snow-white sail on a velvet sea.

But Dunn was already popping frogs into the white cloth bag at his waist. The scientist was wasting no time in poetic fancy. He was busy hunting up new species, tuning his ear to catch a strange voice among the voices of thousands, and pouncing upon a rare find, as though it were a treasure of antiquity.

We returned for dinner quite late. It was always a pleasure to see the clean, cool native servants padding around the dining room, so quietly, on bare feet. They were not fat, like the Dutch. They had trim, supple figures, both men and women. They were agile, they moved easily, gracefully, quietly, exhibiting that undulating motion of the hips which all people who practise carrying loads on the head seem to possess. But there is something unfathomable about these Javanese, something in their eyes when you speak to them that tells you that you could never hope to reach their understanding, that their mind is of a different fabric, capable through some mysterious power, perhaps, of undermining the strength of the great Dutch Government itself.

As soon as I received an answer from the Governor-general's aide, B. and I motored up about a hundred miles to Tjipanas. My interview with his Excellency could not have been more satisfactory. He simply asked me what he could do for me, and I did not hesitate to tell him. Within five minutes he had presented me with the S. S. *Dog*, a four hundred ton government boat, for a period of two months, and letters of introduction to all the residents of the Sunda Islands, Banda, and Celebes. And all because the Dutch are genuinely desirous of helping scientific expeditions and because we had been formally introduced through diplomatic channels.

A few days later we were piling into a launch, bag and baggage, in the roadstead of Batavia, ready to go aboard the *Dog*. I felt like the baker, in the "Hunting of the Snark,"—"with 42 boxes all carefully packed, with his name painted clearly on each." But, at least, I had the wit to "mention the fact," so that they were not "all left behind on the beach."

Shortly afterward, we were steering down the coast of Java towards Sourabaya. The sea was rough and choppy. Defosse collapsed in short order, followed in succession by Lee Fai, B., and Chu. However, in two days the agony was over, and we were putting in our last supplies at the largest seaport in the Indies.

CHAPTER IV

A VOLCANO, NUDITY AND TIGERS

"AND THEY CAME UNTO A LAND IN WHICH
IT SEEMED ALWAYS AFTERNOON."

On Friday, June 4th, at 6 P.M., we set sail from Sourabaya. The Straits of Madura were quite calm, the air cool and pleasant, and all on board enjoyed a sumptuous dinner. At last we had really started on our rather adventurous undertaking, and, no doubt, with our starting, some big lizard in a distant jungle stirred uneasily with a sense of fate advancing.

Could anything more ideal be imagined than a private yacht—for that is virtually what the Government boat amounted to—on which to cruise among unfrequented islands of the Southern Seas? The cool, soft air of summer soothed us gently as night fell on the ocean, and I could not help thinking, when the engine throbbed and the foam whispered around our bow, that "the sweetest way to me is a ship's upon the sea." It seemed, indeed, that we were enjoying the very springtime of life. After supper I strolled aft, and stood leaning over the stern rail watching a wake of phosphorescent light that appeared to reflect the powdered vault overhead. Then I looked aloft, into that great galaxy of galaxies, musing

PHOTO BY MRS. BURDEN

A silhouette of the famous dancing girls of Den Passear.

the while on the infinity of the heavens and our own finite existence. "If they be inhabited," those endless starry skies, "what a world of suffering: if they be uninhabited, what a waste of space!" How bound in we are by an anthropocentric point of view! It was time to philosophize, however, and enjoy life, for we had made a final break with civilization.

Early the next morning, after a delicious sleep on deck, we looked out upon the Idgin Mountains of eastern Java, said to possess the largest crater in the world. From the sea it was a remarkable spectacle, remarkable not only on account of the natural beauty of the long, undulating lower slopes and the heaving and falling crest line of the crater's rim, but chiefly on account of the gigantic volcano that could so easily be reconstructed in one's imagination, and the mental picture of the appalling eruption that had once shattered the world, causing unthinkable devastation, and hurling many cubic miles of rock into the sky. The hidden, subterranean forces necessary to accomplish such an explosion are beyond understanding. More than half of the whole mountain had been hurled into space. It should not be a difficult matter to determine along certain physiographic principles the original outline of this gigantic volcano whose summit was probably once glistening under a blanket of snow, the apex of the cone possibly exceeding an altitude of 17,000 feet.

After luncheon I went up onto the bridge with Capt. Knijff. Knijff was a fine skipper and every inch a gentleman. He was a pleasure to be with. Presently as we looked into the distance an island rose out of the sunlit sea. First a cloud-capped volcano, then luxuriant slopes, and finally white strips of glistening sand came up over the horizon. It was Bali—a lazy, languorous island that seemed to be steeped in the heat and haze of that equatorial afternoon. Just as I first saw it, so will I always think of it—"a land in which it seemed always afternoon."

We rowed ashore under a glare that burnt the eye-balls, and ambled, or rather, shuffled, negrolike, through the streets of Boeleling. The shade of a rest-house beckoned, so we sat ourselves down wearily and swallowed a glass of beer. You can feel Bali. The atmosphere of it permeates to the bones. But to feel it is not enough; one must look, also. So, under the influence of the cool draughts of lager, we began to open our eyes. Bali has many attractions. Not the least of these is the nudity, which I should pronounce the most striking feature of an altogether pleasing landscape.

Bright green paddy fields, and palm trees glistening in the sunshine, alluring, thatched villages sleeping in the shade of cocoanut groves, combined with the lack of wearing apparel, melt together so harmoniously against a background of sapphire seas, luxuriant fields, and cloud-capped volcanoes, that it is, indeed, not surprising that the fame of Bali has spread to the ends of the earth. But to return to the nudity, which is really astonishing in both its quantity and quality. There are women, women, everywhere, such round, plump partridges, yet so lithe and graceful, and exhibiting such perfection of form as to inspire the artist.

We passed a village absurd in its picturesqueness, with the tiny palm leaf huts hidden behind moss-covered clay walls. We peeped through enchanting old thatched doorways that led into clean-swept earthen yards that were drowsing in the shade of great banyan trees. At every turn we came upon age-old temples buried in verdure, where the sweetness of the sacred tube-rose, which is grown in all the holy places of Bali, perfumes the air. Here the Hindu religion still holds sway, and the amazing, stone-carved gateways which form such striking and prominent architectural features, are from their weird beauty, a constant joy to the traveller.

In one of these temples we saw the famous dancing-girls.

Though only ten years old, they went through the most amazing gyrations. Bound up, they were, like two little mummies, in brilliantly colored brocades, their head-dresses of solid gold, filled with the sacred lotus flower. Picture these exotic painted little creatures, sitting like statues under the shade of a giant waringan tree. Behind them are some twenty golden instruments which with a sudden burst of fascinating music brings the small dancers to life. They twist and turn in such marvellous contortions as only a child can achieve. All the dancers are trained from babyhood, but must stop as soon as they reach puberty. Each dance is symbolic and recounts some ancient Hindu legend. They last for thirty or forty minutes, during which every muscle is brought into the most exquisite play. One of the children was a real paragon, and would rank with the best dancers of any land. It was all flat-footed, on uneven ground, yet the grace, control and suppleness were incomparable.

At twilight we hid by a mossy pool, and watched an entire village come wandering, one by one, down the leafy paths to bathe. There is no false modesty in Bali, and men and women bathe together in a state of nature, with perfect unconcern. The maidens, those exquisite, but rather shy bronze water nymphs, wash and prink and comb their long jet black hair, and indulge themselves in the Eastern sport of big game hunting through the wilderness of a friendly scalp; and then, rather languidly, they gird up their loins with the inevitable sarong, fill the water jars, set them gracefully on their heads, and move quietly off through the dark vistas of the jungle. The men, on the other hand, go about the business of washing somewhat more vigorously.

For several days we wandered through the matchless isle of Bali, which is still untrammeled by Westerners, undisturbed by European civilization.

Then we set to work collecting reptiles and amphibians. We pitched camp in the tiger country of western Bali, or perhaps more properly it should be called, monkey land, from the millions of monkeys that swarm everywhere through the forest. Collecting, however, was very poor; there are very few species, and rather few individuals. So, one fine morning, when we ran onto some large, fresh tiger tracks, we determined to spend a few days hunting the great striped cat.

Tiger hunting, as it is done in Bali, is a nervous business. The first morning after the bait had been put out, I crept through the jungle at dawn toward the leafy blind which we had constructed, in order to facilitate our approach unseen. The tiger had just left. I therefore installed myself in the boma, or "tempat mendjaga," that is, watching place, as the natives call it, and waited. The boma consisted of a mere screen of leaves about eight yards from the foul-smelling bait. Usually, a tiger returns for a feast a couple of times during the day, but on this occasion, of course, he did not, so I was there twelve hours, unable to move. The torture of it cannot be imagined. Of course, I kept thinking that I heard him coming, and that kept my nerves on edge. Then I got a back ache, a neck ache, a headache, and I knew that if I moved or made any noise, it might spoil the whole show.

One soon develops a mania to bag a tiger, especially if one is thwarted. Of course, this keenness may turn to dread, as B. admitted, when faced with one's first tiger, at not more than ten yards. "I am pretty confident of my dear Mannlicher," she wrote, "but it will take a steady hand even at close quarters to hit so small a mark as the brain with my first shot. Defosse says that some of the best shots shake so that they miss tigers at three or four yards. I picture every emergency day and night, which only makes me more anxious to be pulling the trigger."

B. was, indeed, surprised at her own enthusiasm.

"I can't understand myself," she wrote, "for I fail to see what pleasure there can be in sitting all day scrunched up in a boma waiting for a tiger to come and devour some dead animal whose smell is almost overpowering. Then there are so many painful moments. Even now, as I write in camp, I am very uncomfortable. It is night. The moon is rising over distant hills. The jungle all around me is filled with strange sounds, and D. is away at one of the baits where a tiger came last night. Of course, one always feels confident about one's own safety, and even about another person's, when one is with him; but the minute D. is off alone for long, my imagination runs away with me. There are no horrors I have not been through at such times. Thank goodness, I can hear him coming at last, with the coolies yelling to scare off the tigers, that frequently follow in their footsteps at night. These Malays are terrified after dark, and so was I, until I heard them coming just now, for a tiger roared quite close by—a blood-curdling sound. Chu and I are alone in camp, and I think he is pretty nervous, too. He talks loudly and piles dry leaves on the fire.

"I am afraid that what I took for the coolies was only night birds, screaming in the distance. I can write no more until D. gets back.

"Now a shot has gone off close by. He must have stopped off at one of the baits on his way home, and killed a tiger. It's so dark, though! I hope to heaven that he has not just wounded the beast!"

But, in reality, when we arrived in camp, the coolies were only carrying a deer which had been shot for meat.

B. told me what a miserable time she had had waiting, and yet, somehow, she said, she wouldn't miss this hunting for anything. Of course, one changes entirely when one enters the jungle. A few days ago we were wandering sluggishly around, indifferent to almost everything—typical white people of the tropics, and then, all of a sudden, upon entering the jungle, we had come to life again. We were alert, keen, interested. We walked miles every day, and were busy all the time. Defosse, too, was in his element, and looked like a different man, altogether.

The next morning, Defosse and B. started for the tiger bait, well before dawn, as they wanted to reach it with the first streak of light.

"We had not gone a hundred yards from camp," she wrote, "before something crashed off into the underbrush on our right. I said nothing, but clung closer to Defosse, who carried the only light, which shed fantastic shadows on the path, whilst on all other sides was a thick wall of darkness.

"Deeper and deeper we went into that black, breathless forest, and I felt sure that we were being lured on to our destruction by some stealthy, slinking thing, padding noiselessly ahead. Here, 'wait a-bit' thorns stretched out clutching fingers, and I thought of Defosse's story of the hunter who ran into some of these when charged by a tiger, and came out the other side with every stitch of clothes torn from his body, and most of his skin, as well. Then, suddenly, the light caught and flashed two glowing eyes, which seemed malevolently to bar the way. I cocked my rifle to shoot, but Defosse said, 'No, a deer,' and it bounded away. Once more, I breathed freely and so moved on—this time with no headlight, and with greatest caution, as we were nearing the bait. Now we stopped again and listened. The first grey streak of dawn was creeping down through the tree-tops and we shivered in our dew-drenched clothes, as we waited until we could see our sights. Then as we advanced, our way was heralded by the disturbed chirpings of awakened bird-life, while the distant grumblings of monkeys proclaimed more fearful marauders to be abroad. In fact, all the forest life seemed to be conspiring against us to give warning of our approach. On the other hand, we had the dew to be thankful for. Branches cracked dully under foot. The tall grass in the open glades whispered very softly as we moved through it, and the leaves that usually rustled like a field of corn now hung limply, as if sound asleep.

"Then, as we drew nearer, I distinctly heard the low grumblings and grunting of a tiger on the bait. We knew that one had been there about this hour the day before, so on I crept, alone this time, my heart in my mouth, fully prepared to meet our foe, face to face.

"Now I was only forty yards from the blind, and the bait was out of sight, not ten yards beyond the small barricade of leaves. Was that the tip of the tiger's tail that caught my eye? Was he lying there by the bait, his sleek body stretched out along the ground, his amber eyes fixed suspiciously on the blind behind which I moved? 'How cold it seems in this gloomy jungle! Or is it the cold that makes my limbs tremble so unpleasantly when I stop to listen? But I mustn't stop that way—bad for the nerves. What was that?—Oh, yes, big wings beating heavily on still air: hornbills passing overhead—lucky birds! Wretched business, this not being able to see the tiger until you almost step on him, and—look, there, he has been using our trail—what huge pads! No, I must not stop again.'

"Now the time had come; I raised myself gently until I could look through the peep-hole, then slowly I turned towards Defosse, and slowly shook my head. I did not know whether to be more relieved or sorry that there was nothing but a big black boar tearing ravenously at the bait. That was my first tiger!

A black wall of fresh steaming lava from the volcano of Batur.

"After that we settled ourselves in the 'tempat mendjaga,' to wait for El Tigre. He was sure to come back at any moment, so, again and again I fitted my rifle into the aperture made for it and aimed at various points of our unfortunate cow's anatomy. This cow, by the way, had been dead for four days, so that putrefaction had reached its limit. The whole carcass seemed to move with the writhing mass of corruption that filled it, and the smell, combined with the heat, and the discomfort of our position, was almost insupportable. Then, mosquitoes and ants began their voracious biting, in spite of which we dared not move a finger. Meanwhile, my nerves were stretched to breaking point, listening and watching for some sign of the approaching tiger. First a twig cracked like a pistol shot behind us, and I waited to see a great tawny head come pushing through our flimsy barrier. Of what use, then, our rifles. Next, a far-off rustling sound came ever nearer, until a band of monkeys swung chattering and grumbling into the trees above us. This is often a sign that a tiger is lurking somewhere near, or has even carried off one of their number.

"Once more we waited in vain, and, as the heat of noon drew near, the jungle seemed to hold its breath with us—listening. Not a leaf stirred to break that sunlit stillness. Then, just as we had about reached the limit of our endurance, my heart suddenly stood still at the unmistakable sound of distant, stealthy footsteps. First they seemed to come from one side, and then another—occasionally pausing, and then padding relentlessly forward, until I realized to my horror that they were coming from directly behind us. We would have to sit motionless while the beast passed by within a few inches, unable to see anything of him until he was actually on the bait. My nerves cried out at the thought!

"On, on, they came—those ominous footsteps for what seemed a lifetime, and then, suddenly, they were upon us. I could even hear the great beast breathing as he paused beside our shelter. Why, in heaven's name, did he not pass on toward the bait? My rifle lay cocked and ready, and I prayed for the strength to shoot it when the time came. Did I imagine that glittering eye that seemed to be peering in at us through the leaves? He seemed intent upon torturing us, for it must have been at least ten minutes that we sat thus, before he once more moved forward into our sight. Then I saw a big black head, instead of a yellow one, followed by a long, snake-like body. My gun slipped from my nerveless fingers, and Defosse and I faced each other with the one word of 'salvator' on our lips. Our bait had drawn one of the largest of these big lizards ever seen. That was my second tiger, the last for one day."

His Royal Highness had no intention of visiting the bait during daylight, so that it became necessary to build a platform in a nearby tree, in order to do some night hunting. From the platform an electric light could be turned on, which would shine on the bait. A tiger moving through the jungle does not make the slightest sound. The first warning of his presence, therefore, would be the sound of crunching bones. Then, while he was in the midst of his feast, I could switch on the light, and shoot in the same breath.

However, as luck would have it, this austere being crept through the jungle and observed the coolies as they were building the platform. The coolies were shouting back and forth to each other, and Defosse, who was prowling around, looking for rattan vines, nearly ran into him.

After that, he kept his distance, and, though I spent two entire nights drowsing uncomfortably on my little narrow platform in the pitch black jungle, I never had a shot.

So, as time was short, we disconsolately sailed up the

coast in a native prau. As we approached Boeleling, we became vaguely conscious of low rumblings, like thunder. On arriving, the rumblings were much more noticeable, and we were told that the volcano of Batur was in eruption, that lava was pouring down the mountain side, and that the village of Batur had been annihilated.

The opportunity was certainly too good to miss—a volcano in eruption was not to be seen every day. We therefore proceeded immediately, an hour by motor, to the rest house of Kintamani, situated at 5000 feet, on the rim of the caldera.

During the ascent it got colder and colder, and darker and darker, until we were finally immersed in a thick, damp cloud. We were chilled to the bone, and, as it was impossible to see, progress was hazardous, to say the least. At a turn of the road, another car ran into us, but the accident proved fatal neither to the car nor to its occupants, and we proceeded again hesitatingly. White, choking mist drove by in gusts. The monsoon shrieked above the mountain tops. Streams of refugees from the destroyed village passed us, single file. Then darkness came down, and still we had not reached the rest house. The constant booming and the explosions were getting louder and louder. It was quite thrilling, this night ride through a cloud toward an erupting volcano. B. stated that we were perfect fools, that it was a nonsensical thing to do, and that we ought to be headed in the opposite direction. But I knew that she was enjoying the excitement of it, just the same. Then, of a sudden, the fog lifted for a moment. On the left, as the vapor rolled away from under our feet, we became aware of a great abyss, a yawning gulf, which groaned with dull and intermittent roars.

We were on the rim of a crater, and below us was the ancient caldera within which the young cone of Batur had been formed. Suddenly a golden glow illuminated the banks of fog. Streamers of water vapor in fantastic shapes scurried this way

A jewel of an emerald isle.

and that, in the eddying currents of wind. Then they parted, these wisps of fog, and we saw, down in that yawning abyss, perhaps the greatest wonder of the world—a volcano in action. Half the mountain of Batur seemed to be in flames. A giant rift in the mountain's side showed the line of weakness in its superficial crust, through which the fountains of lava hurled themselves into the darkness. Blood red against the blackness of night, this lava threw itself hundreds of feet into the air, and showered back to earth, there to join the slowly grinding flow, which, with irresistible force, crept down the lower slopes of the cone. The bombardment now was terrifying, explosion following explosion in rapid succession. Just then, our motor pulled up at a miserable little shanty, that gave the impression of being lost in the night. It was the rest house—a cold, wet, poorly illuminated structure of boards, in which the window panes rattled and broke with the force of the detonations.

After a miserable, cold, dreary night, during which we enjoyed fitful slumbers and listened to the never ending outbursts of the erupting volcano, we walked down the steep inner slope of the caldera toward the fresh lava flows, which still moved relentlessly forward, sprawling over the plain at the base of the cone. Sometimes the lava surged rapidly forward, a mass of molten magma and black cinders, covering a distance of two miles in an hour, but more usually it rolled forward at an almost imperceptible pace. The surface was a jagged mass of black porous rock, with streams of smoke and gas rising from it, here and there. In places it glowed deep red for a moment. So grim a field of desolation and ruin cannot be described. We approached the edge of the ragged flow which stood before us—a black wall of hot and twisted rock, twenty-five feet high. From a point of vantage, we looked over the desolate plain, with its wisps of yellow smoke and white steam. Not far off, the site of the village of Batur could be plainly distinguished. Only the

64

Two sisters of Den Passear.

temple—built on a small hill—still stood erect, and yet even this sacred abode of the Gods was momentarily threatened with destruction. A few roofs of temple buildings could still be seen above the lava, but the rest of the village of two thousand inhabitants no longer existed.

Yet all this was as nothing in impressiveness, when compared with the innumerable dull red fountains that streamed skyward from the rift in the volcano's side. And, with each deluge of magma that was hurled aloft, came a sound like the bursting of giant bombs. Field-glasses in hand, I observed the masses of lava glass of all sizes change shape in the air, cool perceptibly, and then fall like hail on every side, thus forming what is known as a cinder cone. From each vent, subterranean explosions threw up lava, gas, volcanic bombs and other ejecta, constantly. At every second, millions of missiles were hurled into the air, while millions of others fell on every side. In this way, many miniature, or parasitic cones and craters were in the act of formation on the side of the volcano of Batur. And so it is that, by explosions of a gas-charged basaltic lava, the great chain of the Lesser Sunda Islands has been built up from under the sea, bit by bit, through hundreds of thousands of years. It is a marvelous thing to see a constructional landform actually in the process of construction.

But where does the lava that has formed this great chain of islands come from? Why and how does it make its way to the surface? To begin with, all the volcanoes of Java and the Lesser Sunda group have been formed along the axis of the so-called Sunda fold, a great arc in the earth's crust, extending for over three thousand miles, from Sumatra to the Philippines. The alignment of volcanoes along the arc is due to abyssal fissuring. The fissuring, which extends from the earth's surface to the basaltic substratum at a depth of forty miles, is due to tension within the crust of lighter rocks. Basaltic lava from the

A Hindu temple in Bali. The temple gateways form the most characteristic and prominent architectural features of this beautiful and luxuriant island.

substratum then wells up along the fissure, finally to be discharged at the surface, as a result of the process of "gas fluxing." According to Daly, "on the principle of the uncorked soda water bottle, the magma in the chamber is effervescing."—" As the bubbles rise to levels of ever-decreasing pressure, they expand, become still more buoyant, and move all the faster: and they bring their heat with them."—"We shall not be surprised, therefore, if the expanding, composite mass of liquid and gas jumps, fountain-like, into the air, some distance."

However, it seems that the rising gas in the magma chamber moves rhythmically. "Periods of abundant emanation alternate with periods of sparse emanation." This rhythmical periodicity would account for the regularity of the eruptions of Batur, which have occurred at exactly ten-year intervals as far back as the natives can remember. During a period of quiet, the magma in the volcano's vent becomes solidified into a plug. Hot gas slowly accumulates beneath the plug, and when the pressure of gas is sufficiently great, a major explosion takes place. "The plug, and, it may be, much of the surrounding rock, are blown into the air." The strength of an explosion then depends upon the resistance of the lava plug to the pent-up forces beneath. If the plug is small, it acts as a safety valve, allowing the volcano to ease itself periodically. If the plug is very resistant, the increasing pressure will eventually produce a shattering explosion, such as occurred at Krakatoa, in 1883, when the whole island was destroyed.

It was a great opportunity at Batur, to witness this most interesting phenomenon. I was sorry to leave. As we sped away down the long lower slopes of the mountain, through entrancing villages, surrounded by the beautiful scenery of that garden island, we could still hear Batur roaring and rumbling in the distance, as if threatening us with annihilation, and, in truth, annihilation is just what would have overtaken us all,

A golden hued daughter of Bali snapped in a temple gateway.

had Batur lake suddenly emptied itself, as well it might have, into the bowels of the earth. Verily, an erupting volcano is one of the most awe-inspiring of nature's wonders.

In a few hours we were aboard *The Dog*, sailing away toward the rising sun. I have seen many "jewels of the orient," and "garden spots of the East," but certainly, none possesses quite the charm that belongs to Bali. Bali is a toyland of cocoanut groves, in which all of man's contrivances seem to have been built more for their pleasing appearance than for their usefulness. Every prospect tries to be alluring. Farewell, beautiful island! You typify the longed-for land of sunshine and beautiful women, that white men dream of.

CHAPTER V

A FORGOTTEN ISLAND

THE beautiful unbroken crest-line of Gunung Agung and the cone of Batur could still be seen in the distance, when *The Dog* plunged and danced into Lombok Strait.

The wind racing through the cut between Bali and Lombok drove the seas down upon us in short, steep ridges of black water, so that we tossed and churned merrily on our way; not so merrily, however, for those who found nothing but a terrible giddiness in the sickening lurches of the good ship *Dog*. The Captain assured us that she was a remarkably seaworthy vessel, designed by a master hand; but then, as Defosse said, in a very disgruntled tone of voice (for he was having much the worst of it), "Every captain feels toward his ship as a father toward his child." However, though she left much to be desired in the way of comfort, *The Dog* was a staunch, sturdy little craft, brave enough to weather any gale. The native crew were as thick as rats on board, and fairly swarmed over the deck. In fact, everything took place on one little deck, which served as kitchen, dining-room, bed-room and bath.

However, we were crossing the famous "Wallace's Line," so there was something else to think about. Alfred Russel Wallace was a great naturalist and a great traveller. He lived in the East Indies for over eight years, voyaging in native praus

thousands upon thousands of miles through that great archipelago. Like any traveller in the tropics, he was frequently
stricken with malaria. On one of these occasions, when he was
in bed, tormented with a raging fever, and aching eye-balls, the
magnificent conception of the evolution of life flashed across
his mind. What amazing lucidity in such circumstances! He
has recorded in his autobiography this great moment in his
life. Already, he had done work that was destined to make his
the great name in the Malay Archipelago; now he was assuring his title to honor, along with Darwin, for the discovery of
evolution:

> "At the time in question I was suffering from a sharp
> attack of intermittent fever, and every day, during the cold
> and succeeding hot fits, had to lie down for several hours,
> during which time I had nothing to do but to think over
> any subjects then particularly interesting to me. One day
> something brought to my recollection *Malthus's Principles
> of Population*, which I had read about twelve years before.
> I thought of his clear exposition of 'positive checks to
> increase,'—disease, accidents, war, and famine—which
> keep down the population of savage races to so much
> lower an average than that of more civilized people. It
> then occurred to me that these causes or their equivalents
> are continually acting in the case of animals also; and,
> as animals usually breed much more rapidly than does
> mankind, the destruction every year from these causes
> must be enormous in order to keep down the numbers of
> each species, since they evidently do not increase regularly
> from year to year, as otherwise the world would long
> ago have been densely crowded with those that breed
> most quickly. Vaguely thinking over the enormous and
> constant destruction which this implied, it occurred to
> me to ask the question, Why do some die, and some live?
> And the answer was clearly, that on the whole, the best

fitted live. From the effects of disease, the most healthy
escaped; from enemies, the strongest, the swiftest, or the
most cunning; from famine, the best hunters, or those
with best digestion; and so on. Then it suddenly flashed
upon me that this self-acting process would necessarily
improve the race, because in every generation the inferior
would inevitably be killed off and the superior would
remain—that is, the *fittest would survive*. The more I
thought it over, the more I became convinced that I had at
length found the long-sought for law of nature that solved
the problem of the origin of species. For the next hour I
thought over the deficiencies in the theories of Lamarck
and of the author of *Vestiges*, and I saw that my new theory
supplemented these views and obviated every important
difficulty. I waited anxiously for the termination of my
fit so that I might at once make notes for a paper on the
subject. The same evening I did this pretty fully, and on
the two succeeding evenings wrote it out carefully, in
order to send it to Darwin by the next post, which was to
leave in a day or two."[1]

Thus, Wallace, quite independently, was reaching the
same conclusion that Darwin was reaching on the other side
of the world. Later, these two great men corresponded on the
subject, each trying to make the other take the credit.

But, as I said a moment ago, we were crossing "Wallace's
Line." Primarily, it is a demarcation line between a deep and
a shallow sea. In a broader sense, however, Wallace took it as
a dividing line between two of the basic faunas of the world;
namely, the Asiatic fauna, which extends down into Sumatra,
Java, and Borneo (for these islands in very recent geological
time-probably during the last glacial period-were a part of the
mainland of Asia), and the Australian fauna, characterized by
marsupials, which has spread northward into New Guinea and
the Timor group. Recent investigation, however, has shown

[1] ALFRED RUSSEL WALLACE: *MY LIFE: A RECORD OF EVENTS AND OPINIONS*, PP. 361-363

that it is impossible to draw as exact a boundary as Wallace supposed between these faunal divisions, and that, as a matter of fact, there is a large belt, trending north and south, in which both faunas intermingle in varying proportions. Fuller research has simply widened the "Line" into a broad belt. Komodo falls within this belt, and, for that reason, it is perhaps a logical place for the largest of all lizards to have survived

The southeast Trades began blowing up harder than ever, so that, in spite of the blue sky, the water had such a dark, sinister look about it as the combers raced by, that I began to feel rather uncomfortable.

When the sun set, there occurred quite a remarkable phenomenon which I had never noticed before. For a moment, the sun hung on the horizon, glowing sullenly down a long, shimmering pathway of heaving waters. Then, as the last crescent-like tip took a farewell peek across the sea, a beautiful, pale green light shone for the fraction of a second, and was gone. In all probability, it was an optical illusion, or, rather, after-image, in which the complementary color asserted itself.

That night, as we passed Alas Strait, the sea had no mercy on us. Black water pounded in over the bow and slewed around the decks with the roar of a mountain torrent. It was terrifying for B., who expected to be washed away with each crashing wave that swept over us. "The smashing seas," she wrote, "seemed completely to submerge our little vessel, and I lay quaking most of the night, with my head splitting with the roar of wind and water." Small wonder that B. was nervous, waking up out of a sound sleep into such a world. *The Dog* was being unmercifully battered, and such were the gyrations of the craft that, at 2 A.M., I went to see how the rest of the party were faring. Lee Fai and Chu were dead to the world, too weak and sick to give audible answer, but Defosse was groaning and tossing in agony. He thought his kidneys had ceased to function, and, what with the pain that was shooting up his back, he was fairly writhing on his cot. I gave him a good dose of codein to relieve his suffering. Dunn was sleeping peacefully; he alone, enjoyed oblivion. After that I crawled up to the Captain's cabin, where I found the master of the ship calmly reading a novel. He had already reduced our speed, and was content, therefore, to let us wallow in the high seas.

In the morning, we came into the lee of Sumbawa, and passed under the brow of majestic Tomboro. The old volcano exploded, or rather, blew its head off, in 1815, destroying 12,000 people. The crater, I was told, is now filled by a lake. What a relief, to have some mountains interposing their broad backs between us and the trade winds! It is interesting to note that, according to Playfair's "law of maximum rotation," the southeast Trades of this region become, on crossing the Equator, the southwest monsoon, of the China Sea. The wind takes an almost right-angle turn at the Equator. In June, the southeast Trade is not steady, but in July it sets in to blow without respite, a relentless, merciless semi-gale, and I was mighty glad not to be out in *The Dog* on the south side of the Lesser Sunda Islands. The air, as we progressed eastward, was getting cooler, which signified, perhaps, that it was being blown up from more temperate climes far to the south. Also, I noticed a certain yellow light in the atmosphere, said to be caused by suspended dust from the Australian desert. Thus, the wind also helps to destroy a continent. Fortunate it is for us, that continents are dominantly rising bodies—the lighter rocks of which they are composed floating up, as it were, on a heavier basaltic substratum,[2] else they would have ceased to exist long ago. The waves are attacking their shorelines, crumbling them away. Rivers are eating the very hearts out of their great mountains, and even the wind has joined forces, and is scattering particles of land over the high seas.

---

[2] THE THEORY OF THE FLOATING CONTINENTS IS STILL FOR LACK OF EVIDENCE THEORETICAL.

The green turtles of the Pacific, Chelonia agassizii, caught by natives on the east coast of Sumbawa.

In the evening, we swung south into the beautiful bay of Bima. Glassy water with shimmering reflections stretched away tantalizingly on every side, and, beyond that, sunkissed shores, fringed with leaning palm trees, and long, mellow slopes tanned by the sun, beckoned silently. As we neared the meeting-point of land and sea, everyone became vastly excited. We saw wild horses and buffaloes in great numbers on the flanks of the mountains. We trotted out several pairs of field glasses, and vied with each other in spying game. Defosse, who had been suffering the tortures of the damned a few hours before, gradually came to life. First, he stretched himself, then he sat up and looked around sleepily, then he saw something that interested him, and called for a pair of binoculars, and the next moment he was leaning over the rail, pointing at all the objects that excited his attention. We steamed up the inlet as dusk fell, and cast anchor off the little village of Bima. When it was quite dark, we rigged a light overboard and caught a few of the millions of strange creatures that inhabit tropical seas. These included an eel, squids, pipe fish, sharks, etc., etc. It was good sport netting them as they swarmed up under the light.

The next morning, I went ashore to see the Assistant Resident and the Raja Bechara, in order to arrange about securing natives to accompany us to Komodo. In striking contrast to the beautiful inlet is the ugliness of Bima itself. It is a small town, disheveled and unhealthy. Its unkempt, dirty appearance, and the horrible corrugated tin roofs reminded me vaguely of Bluefields, Nicaragua, the most depressing town I have ever set foot in.

The Assistant Resident, a very cordial gentleman with a keen interest in natural history, received me with every courtesy and consideration. He had heard of our expedition and was ready to facilitate our preparations with everything at his command. Accordingly, he summoned the Raja Bechara, a rather fat, lazy, unattractive individual, dressed in khaki, and politely instructed him to procure for us fifteen stalwart bush-men and a headman, or mandoor, to command them. Nobody from Sumbawa had ever visited Komodo, so there was no ques-tion of finding guides who knew the country. It appeared that we would have to steam around to Telok Sapi (Cow Bay) in eastern Sumbawa, where the Raja would be ready for us with a select group of Malays. Then, the business concluded, the Assistant Resident began to ask me some questions about the Komodo lizards. What was so interesting about them? Why were they worth coming so far to get? I answered, first of all, by saying that they were the last great find that a naturalist could make; that they were at once of great spectacular inter-est and of real scientific value. Except for the original descrip-tion of Ouwens, who had never been to Komodo, it was an unknown beast. Even its relationships had not been definitely determined. The Assistant Resident was very much interested. We discussed dragon stories and the origin of dragon stories. I told him of the importance of the dragon in the mythology of almost every country in the world. This mythical saurian has figured frequently in the folk-lore of peoples in every quarter of the globe. Moreover, it is interesting to note that the various descriptions of the beast have a striking resemblance to each other; so much so, that it seems quite incredible that they could have arisen independently out of thin air. Dragon stories must originally have been founded on fact; that is, on some beast that actually lived, a giant, carnivorous lizard, perhaps, whose size and strength and voracious habits were such as properly to impress the mind of primitive man. So strong was the belief in dragons, even in comparatively recent times, that many pic-tures have been painted of mail-clad princes mounted on some trusty stallion dashing gallantly to the rescue of a beautiful whiteskinned maiden who was about to be torn to pieces. The imperial Chinese flag used the dragon as a symbol of national strength.

The dragon was always pictured with a long, forked tongue, powerful jaws, and gigantic claws with which he would rend his victims asunder. A fiery dragon in itself is a fascinating idea—so, also, is the thought of a beautiful white-skinned maiden. Link these two ideas together, in some way or other, and you have a story which by its very nature would survive through untold ages.

"Well," said the Assistant Resident, "you have something to look forward to, then. You are about to indulge in the sport of legendary princes. You will have a remarkable story to tell."

"Exactly," I answered; "it is just possible that the Komodo lizards are the very ones which have given rise to all the dragon mythology."

With that, I thanked him profusely for his kind assistance, and left him pondering the question in silence, for no doubt it seemed strange to him that we had come all the way from New York to find out something about animals that lived within a day's travel from his headquarters. Perhaps he was beginning to wonder why he had not been to Komodo himself.

Early the following morning we anchored in the beautiful bay of Sapi, off the quaint little village of the same name. The water was a light emerald color, and everywhere fish were jumping over its glassy surface. Looking ashore, I saw a fleet of dugouts being paddled out in our direction. There were sixteen natives already waiting for us, and a wild and picturesque crew they made as they drew alongside and came on board. Their mouths were stained blood-red from chewing betel nut and their teeth were blackened or gone entirely, so that B. described them as "the roughest-looking set of cut throats imaginable." When they came on board Defosse took charge of them and herded them into the bow.

There were two Badjos from Labuan Badjo, in western Flores, two Bugis from Celebes, ten natives from Sapi, and one mandoor, or headman. All the men, of course, were Malays.

We could not risk entering the rapid tidal streams and poorly charted waters of Linta Strait by night, so that it was necessary to delay starting for Komodo till 3 A.M. the following day.

Meanwhile we went ashore to see the Raja Bechara, to whom we were so much indebted for procuring the men. He considers himself a most exalted person and must, therefore, be treated accordingly; so I invited him to take luncheon with us on board *The Dog*. The result was a rather painful ordeal.

In the afternoon we started for one of the many tempting little islands that surrounded us. The natives of the only village on the island, it appeared, had never seen a white woman before, and crowded around B. in an admiring circle. There they stood, open-mouthed, gaping at her, while she, taking advantage of the opportunity, obtained as many pictures as she wanted. Then some of the men offered to catch some big sea turtles for us. It was very exciting and great sport to watch. First, they drove them into a little bay, then they plunged after them, grabbing them by the flippers under water. The childlike glee with which they went after those turtles, struggled with them, and finally, amid splashes and shouts of triumph, hauled them up on the beach, was indeed a novel and diverting sight. Moreover, it was interesting to note that these green turtles closely resemble the *"concha verde,"* of Central American waters. Here, too, for the first time we saw the famous walking fish (*Periophthalmus*) or mud-skippers, most extraordinary creatures which, by flipping their tails, can jump along the beach at a truly astonishing speed. The pelvic fins, which have migrated forward and now lie anterior to the pectorals, are used much as a gecko uses its adhesive disks. During our travels we saw many species of this peculiar genus. Some live on the mud flats, others in mangrove swamps, still others in fresh water streams. Their protective coloration is so perfect that they are very difficult to see when not moving. I tried to catch some in a little stream. Instead of diving, they preferred to scamper over the water and up among the mangrove roots, frequently climbing for some distance above the ground. Only when hard pressed could they be induced to seek safety in their own element and then frequently they would cling to a stone or root with just their big projecting eyes appearing periscope fashion above the surface.

The most interesting species of all were those that lived on an open, rock-bound coast. A beautiful cliff of naked igneous rock plunged into the sea. At the base of the cliff there was at low tide a mass of rounded boulders on which the waves crashed up in a great confusion of foam. Here, on one large boulder, I noticed a whole troop of these walking or jumping fish. They seemed to be having a great time hopping about the surface of that particular boulder, nibbling at I couldn't make out just what. The extraordinary fact, however, was that the seas were breaking regularly with all their force right on top of that boulder, and I could not understand why all those little fish weren't washed off its smooth surface. As soon as the wave receded there they all still were, hopping around, just as if nothing had happened. I took out my field glasses and watched them more closely. A huge wave was rolling in. The crest of it reared up higher and higher. Then it curled ominously and broke upon the rock. When the wave had already curled above the fish they were still hopping merrily around. When it broke, I still observed no change in their actions, but, as the mass of water was about to fling them up the beach, they all turned suddenly, just in time, and faced the wave. In some uncanny, instinctive way, all those fish seemed to know that they could go on feeding until the very last fraction of a second, when they would suddenly turn and face the rushing water, in line, doubtless hanging on for dear life. I was fascinated, watching them, and wished that I had had a moving picture camera with me at the time. Eventually, as the tide came in, they hopped over to another boulder, where they renewed operations with the same fervor.

On our way back to *The Dog*, I asked the Malays if there were any dugongs or sea cows *(Trichechidae)* in these waters. When they answered in the negative I was much disappointed, and yet, knowing how these people value the tear-drops of the dugong as a love-potion, I was certain that the statement was correct. The child-like belief in the efficacy of the tear drops of these great marine mammals still exists. It is firmly believed that any man carrying such a love-potion, that is, a vial of dugong tear-drops, exerts such a powerful spell over any beautiful woman that she will flee from her husband to seek the charmer's favor. I leave it to my readers to estimate, in pure gold, the value of these drops. Could I but obtain some dugong puppies and teach them to cry, a fortune would be mine.

Now we were shaping our course for Telok Sawa (Python Bay), in eastern Komodo. At last we had set out on the last leg of our long journey. At 8:32 A.M., the island was sighted. That which up to now had appeared as no more than a little black dot on a map of the Dutch East Indies suddenly loomed up before us in full reality—a mass of bulky mountains rising out of the sea. A few wisps of white cloud hung over the island. Already, through my field glasses, I could discern patches of jungle. "So, that was really Komodo!" It hardly seemed possible that we were actually arriving. We were excited inside, and yet conscious of a serenity that we had not expected. Although we had travelled half way around the world and were now in sight of our destination, yet we seemed to take the matter quite for granted, and, after leisurely observing the arid slopes of Komodo, we returned with surprising equanimity to our books.

To be sure, that wily old hunter, Defosse, was itching to stretch his legs on shore. I could tell from the way he was polishing his rifle and fingering the trigger. Dr. Dunn was restlessly fiddling with Shakespeare, while Mrs. B. swung serenely in a hammock, totally oblivious of everything save her book. Lee Fai, with true Chinese conceptions of geography, hadn't the vaguest notion where he was, but rather expected to reach Manila soon. I felt certain that those tenacious explorers who had reached the North and South Poles in the old days of sledge travel must have felt the same on attaining their objective as we did then: "Well, here we are. What now?" It is the endless perversity of human nature that makes it so.

We drew near to Linta Straits, where Wallace tells us that the violent tide rips cause the sea "to boil and foam and dance like the rapids below a cataract, so that vessels are swept about helpless and are sometimes swamped in the finest weather, and under the brightest skies." In the narrow straits of Lolo, between Rindja and Flores, it is even worse. Here the flood tide, backed by a southeasterly wind, sweeps northward at the rate of 13 knots. A more dangerous passage probably does not exist. Already I could see the water boiling ahead, so I ran up onto the bridge.

From this vantage point, one could see everywhere a great commotion in the sea. Islands consisting of upraised coral reefs were dotted about the straits, and I was reminded of those wonderful lines of Holmes:

"The venturous bark that flings
"On the sweet summer wind its purpled wings
"In gulfs enchanted where the siren sings,

"And coral reefs lie bare,
"Where the cold sea-maids rise to sun their
streaming hair."

Just so, we seemed to be, a venturous bark on the sweet summer wind, floating through enchanted gulfs where the coral reefs lie bare.

As we approached ever nearer to Komodo, a few important facts became evident. In the first place, the sailing directions are wrong. Komodo is not limestone. It is volcanic in origin. This may be seen or determined from the typical volcanic necks that form so striking a feature of the landscape. Volcanic necks, or plugs, are formed, as has been explained, by the cooling of molten magma within the vent of a volcano. They are far more resistant to erosion than the cone itself, so that as frequently happens when there is nothing left of the cone, the durable plug, or core, of igneous rock still stands to tell the geologist of the volcano that was once smouldering and booming there. The cycle of erosion on Komodo has reached submaturity. On all the other islands of the Sunda chain visited by the Expedition it is still in a youthful stage. Ordinarily a geologist would not dream of stating that because the erosion cycle had progressed farther on Island A. than on Island B., the former is older; and yet in this particular case I think that the inference can be drawn. For it is evident that as climatic conditions through the Sunda group are uniform and the character of the rock is the same, the rapidity of erosion should be fairly equal.

Komodo has been practically unknown. With the exception of a few pearl fishermen, and the Duke of Mecklenburg, who spent one night there, I did not hear of any white man who had landed on the island before we arrived in June, 1926. Although it is only a small island, twenty-two miles long by twelve miles in width, it fulfilled my wildest dreams. With its sharp serrated skyline, its gnarled mountains, its mellow, sunwashed valleys, and its giant pinnacles that bared themselves like fangs to the sky, it looked more fantastic than the mountains of the moon.

As we drew ever nearer, now jamming through dangerous straits, now skimming past strips of glistening sand that stretched out tantalizingly into the blue translucence of the water, we seemed to see a prehistoric landscape— a lost world—unfold before us. Everywhere, great gubbong palms stood outlined against the blue. It is a melancholy land, a fitting abode for the weird creatures that lived in the dawn of things, and, as such, it seemed to be a suitable haunt for the predatory dragon lizards.

At last, we coasted into the quiet, peaceful waters of Telok Sawa and cast anchor in the lee of a miniature island. Then we went ashore. Upon landing on our longed-for island, I suffered so many impressions that it is impossible to record them all. A stroll along the beach delighted B. and myself, both on account of the beautiful scenes that everywhere met our eyes— each turn unfolding new bits of loveliness—and on account of the prolific fauna of the seashore, so that we soon anticipated many interesting discoveries. Moreover, we were astonished to find how abundant the game was, for, evidently, deer and wild boar were present in countless numbers.

How salubrious was the climate! How deliciously cool— and what a joy it was to stretch our legs on the open beach! For many miles we walked along the edge of the bay, thrilled, after so many months of artificial travel, to be free at last. We could camp any place, we could go anywhere, we could do just as we pleased. That first thrill of getting off into untrodden paths is intoxicating. I felt like running headlong down the beach. B., too, was delighted with everything she saw.

"The sea life," she wrote, "is strange and marvelous,

86

The convict village of Komodo.

ranging through all the colors of the rainbow. The 'sunset crabs' are particularly interesting. Just at this hour one can see thousands of tiny white flags waving beside every stone. One steps closer, and they disappear. After a few minutes' quiet, however, out comes a tiny crab from under each stone, who starts beckoning to his neighbor with one large white claw. These they continue waving until one or the other gives in and sidles to his neighbor's hole. Then begins a real fencing match, with circlings, clashes, and claws frantically beating the air, till, finally, the weaker of the two is pursued, cornered, and dragged down a hole, still gallantly waving his flag."

There is one small village on Komodo, consisting of about forty convicts exported here by the Raja of Sumbawa. They are a degenerate lot of diseased people, that have reached such a degraded state that they don't even seem capable of curiosity. The fact that a steam yacht had entered the bay, perhaps for the first time in history, caused no excitement, and as we approached the cluster of nipa huts, the majority of the inhabitants sneaked into hiding and peeked at us through crevices, like so many helpless, frightened animals. Komodo is a place "where every prospect pleases, and only man is vile."

As we wandered back to the ship, the fresh air was like a tonic from the springs of heaven. A golden sunset painted the rocky islets and the purple sea in glorious colors.

Late at night, I heard tomtoms beating across the water; incessant, monotonous, rhythmic beats, thrilling and barbarous. A native prau was in the bay, and with the aid of drums, the Malays were summoning the winds to blow. It is a common practise for these people before starting on a sea voyage to drum thus, hour after hour, in order to insure a fair breeze. How delightfully child-like and superstitious!

Early next morning, we set out in different directions to

PHOTO BY MRS. BURDEN

*Convicts from the village of Komodo. On the right is an albino
Malay whom at first sight was taken for a leper.*

explore Komodo. It is an arid island, so that, before we could decide where to pitch camp, it was necessary to locate a spot that would combine water and plentiful signs of the big lizards. Accordingly Defosse and Dr. Dunn went northward, and I struck out straight west, across the mountains. Lee Fai spent the day on board in repose, as though he had done nothing but arduous work for months past!

Climbing in the tropics is bad at best, but when the sun is blazing down on a barren hillside, so that the heat rises up again, reflected from the jagged lava rocks, it is little short of torture. One might as well be walking in a furnace. Loose, porous boulders rolled under foot. Saw grass cut the hands. The soles of my boots were torn to pieces and came off at the toes, so that they were flapping at every step. I tied them on with ropes and rawhide, and continued climbing for hours. Eventually I got up into some beautiful, rolling park land, where a cool breeze seemed to descend from the sky. I rested for awhile in the shade of some bamboo. How refreshing it was! Birds were calling in the jungle, sounds so liquid and clear, that in my thirst I was reminded of rocky streams and babbling brooks. Then, as I continued, I saw some wild boar—one trotted by within a few yards of me—and a herd of deer *(Cervus timoriensis)* feeding on a distant slope. A little further on, I came to a pool in the lava rock. Here was an ideal place to camp—good water, a delicious breeze and also a few signs of the giant monitors. Then I went on, to the very summit of the island, and was astonished to see, on the way, the tracks of wild water buffalo *(Bos bubalis)*. Here, then, was an ugly creature I was in no wise prepared to meet, for I had only lead bullets, which would damage him about as much as bird shot. The water buffalo is a formidable antagonist, courageous to a degree almost unknown among other big game animals. Merian Cooper saw a tame bull step deliberately in front of a full grown charging tiger, and toss, him with such frightful strength that 600 pounds of tiger lay bent and broken on the ground. Cooper mercifully dispatched the cat. The brain of a water buffalo is so situated at the back of the skull that a charge is not easily checked by a bullet. Defosse has been on their horns, and still carries the marks on his body today. His escape was miraculous. Water buffalo are usually ranked in danger second only to the elephant, —which seems strange, when one realizes that these cow-like creatures plow the paddy fields of all Asia.

I was wary, therefore, as I followed buffalo trails through patches of jungle, and passed by clumps of thick bamboo. My two coolies were begging me to kill a deer, or *"rusa,"* as they say. *"Tuan pasang rusa"*—"Please, master, shoot a deer." Finally, on sighting a big buck, the temptation was so great that I dropped him with a bullet at the base of the neck. The natives, with endless ejaculations of "oh's" and "ah's" expressed their great astonishment that the white man's rifle would kill at such a distance. It was a good shot, and I was well pleased, inasmuch as it was my first test in many moons.

Then while they were cutting up the deer, I went on up to the divide. Here the view held me spellbound. Everywhere I could look down onto brilliant waters that flashed like a sea of diamonds. It seemed to me that I was standing on the roof of the world, and I felt like Balboa on some lofty peak in Darien.

But it was time to start back. Already I was weary and the strength of the sun, away back on the lava slopes, had given me a headache.

While passing through rolling park land, I was attracted by some big fat blue pigeons, whose voices I heard booming in a patch of thick jungle. As I stepped through the barrier wall of leaves, I noticed another basin in the lava. It was filled with water, and strange to say, two ducks suddenly flew out. Just at that moment I heard a terrific crashing behind me. It sounded as though a whole bamboo forest were being broken into splinters. One of the coolies shouted, *"Carabao!"* (water buffalo) and, in truth, I knew that it could be nothing else. I jumped back, out of the jungle, and just as I emerged into the open, I saw a great solitary bull coming full speed straight towards me. His nose was in the air, his nostrils greatly dilated, and his sweeping horns seemed to be laid back against his flanks. Judging from the speed at which he was coming, he seemed to be charging, although, as I think of it now, I cannot believe that it was more than a coincidence. Although it was a very vivid impression that I obtained of the beast, it was based on no more than one quick glance, for he was less than twenty yards away. I ducked back into the jungle and ran away, displaying, no doubt, great celerity in the act. On the far side of the aforementioned pool was a steep rock, up which I clambered, and there stood with trembling legs, expecting to hear the beast come crashing in at any moment. While wondering what I could do without steel bullets, I suddenly remembered that a water buffalo will not charge into thick jungle. My natives were out of sight. They had vanished suddenly. There was not a sound. The bull must have been standing at the edge of the jungle, some fifteen yards away. In my ignominious position, a few minutes seemed an age, but at last I heard him lumber off at a gallop, his hoofs pounding on the hard ground, till he smashed away into another bamboo thicket. I emerged warily and looked around. Presently the two natives crept out from the jungle. They were very hungry, so they lit a fire and cooked some venison. It was a simple matter, impaling strips of it on sticks and holding it over the blaze, but I was too damned tired to enjoy the feast, and, moreover, my skull felt as though a sledge hammer were at work on it.

At last, just as the evening shadows were gathering, I dragged a weary carcass back to the beach. After months of

The home of the dragon lizard. A glimpse of the rugged mountains of Komodo where climbing under a tropical sun was exhausting work.

an indolent life, the first day in the field is always a hard one. However, we had some beer on board, so that a "sundowner" soon revived me, and we began to compare notes on our first day's adventures.

Defosse and Dunn had found many lizard tracks, and, due to the abundance and variety of game, had had an altogether delightful day. Indeed, if tiger and elephant were on Komodo, the island would be a sportsman's paradise. The game birds included jungle fowl, blue pheasant, five or six different species of pigeon of untold beauty, turtle doves, quail, and a yellow-legged running hen that rather closely resembles the tinamoo of Central America. Moreover, the yellow-crested cockatoos were always in evidence, screaming raucously at each other and flying in every direction over the jungle.

The first day's reconnoitering had been crowned with success, and we had every reason to be elated. Komodo was as interesting an island as it looked, so that after a few hours roaming the wilderness of its rugged slopes, we knew that we could look forward with good reason to many golden days to come.

Our home on Komodo.

CHAPTER VI

DRAGON LIZARDS

THE next day we camped at the head of Telok Sawa. It was an enchanting spot. The whole of our little hut was open to the sea breeze. The roof of woven palm leaves was mellow and bearded with age, and rattled dryly in the wind. All manner of tangled things dangled from it and swayed to and fro; and it concealed the richest assortment of creepy, crawling life, including spiders, scorpions, centipedes, lizards and snakes. The first morning we found a green pit-viper in the roof. Surely a most interesting collection could have been made from this, our shelter.

Inside, it was very comfortable. We built some chairs and a table large enough to hold a lamp, ammunition, note-books, flash-lights, and boxes of every variety. Behind was an upraised bamboo platform, on which we slept.

We had at once put out baits for the *Varanus* and small specimens were already flocking to them in considerable numbers. Dr. Dunn had been watching them all day. He returned in the evening well pleased with the meticulous notes he had taken, stating the exact move of each beast, and the exact time of each move. Lee Fai, who was sent out to take pictures, had only one comment to make: "Walking much trouble!"

Defosse, who still preserved an initial skepticism about

the size of the lizards, cleaned his rifle, pulled his mustache, and made keen, accurate observations on everything he saw, but they always reverted somehow to Indo-China, and not infrequently he drew dubious comparisons between Komodo and the glorious stretch of country northeast of Saigon.

Night fell, and with its falling, the moon rose out of the sea. From where I lay on my bed, I could see the surf pounding on the beach; the incessant roar of it was constantly in our ears.

Next morning I was awakened by a great commotion outside of our hut. I looked up and saw Chu—our priceless Chinese boy—pursuing a pink and black colored beast. He finally secured it in an empty bottle.

"What in the world is it, Chu?" I asked. "Please, Masta, velly bad," was his reply: "all time maka bitie—belong hundred feety." Which, when translated, means that he had captured a large centipede. This loathsome creature we kept captive in order to introduce it into a spider web, and take pictures of whatever happened.

I left camp early and shot a deer for coolie meat. Afterward, I saw many wild boar. And, later still, at 9:30 A.M., at the foot of the pinnacle country on a gently sloping talus cone, covered with short grass and a few palm trees, I saw my first dragon lizard in the open. He was a monster—huge and hoary. I scrambled up to a point of vantage, taking great care, however, not to expose myself, as the eyesight of these beasts is much keener than that of deer. The lizard was working his way slowly down from the mountain crags. The sun slanted down the hill, so that a black shadow pre ceded the black beast as he came. It was a perfectly marvelous sight—a primeval monster in a primeval setting—sufficient to give any hunter a real thrill. Had he only stood up on his hind legs, as I now know they can, the dinosaurian picture would have been com-plete. He stalked slowly and sedately along, obviously hunting for something in the grass, his yellow tongue working incessantly, his magnificent head swinging ponderously this way and that. In my glasses he filled the whole field of vision, and, as there was nothing at hand with which to compare his size, I knew that I could easily and quite faithfully imagine him to be twenty or thirty feet long. These animals are very deceptive. Each one that we saw we thought to be by far the largest, and only after he was dead, and the measuring tape lying along his back, did he shrink to eight or nine feet. Against a background of sunburnt grass, this particular beast of my first encounter looked quite black with age, and I felt sure that he bore the battle scars of many a fierce encounter amid the deep recesses of the isle. Once, and once only, he stopped with his nose buried deep in the grass, as if scenting out some shrew or rat, or small lizard, in order to add another choice morsel to his already distended stomach. Three pigs dashed away at a distance, perhaps to give this great reptile the wide berth he deserved. Then, in some strange fashion he suddenly eluded me and disappeared as completely as if the very earth had swallowed him. Can we but reproduce in the American Museum group the picture I saw that day, the whole expedition will have been worth while.

On my way to camp, my eye lit on the very scenic background for that museum group, a spot which would portray at once the most beautiful and striking features of Komodo. This palm-tree, pinnacle country is, indeed picturesque, but when the traveler is lured among the rugged mountains, he finds that the face of the landscape belies its true character. Walking is extremely arduous, and the deep ravines and gulches harbor all manner of repugnant beasts. Even that morning, one of my barefoot coolies, when about to jump down into a ravine, fortunately looked before he leaped, for, directly beneath him, in the very spot where he would have landed, was a deadly, poisonous viper (*Vipera Russellii*). I had just jumped down to

The "rumah," as the natives call it, of Varanus komodoensis, The deaf beasts use their long claws to excavate these burrows under rocks and tree stumps and retire into them for the night. Notice the native standing at left.

one side, and had not noticed the coiled creature. We caught it alive and removed its fangs.

Shortly after this episode, in the same shaded ravine, I came upon a large cave beneath a tangle of overhanging roots. Such a sequestered nook in the gloom of a dark gulch, is the abode, or "rumah" as the natives call it, of the great lizard. With my left hand I parted some branches, the better to observe the entrance, when suddenly my forearm became red hot. I looked down, and saw that my whole forearm was covered with red ants, —ferocious creatures that are afraid of nothing. So dauntless and predatory are these remarkable insects that they will even bite into the flame of a match until they are consumed by it! I jumped aside, dropping my gun, and for a few minutes experienced an altogether unpleasant sensation.[1]

B. agreed that, although scorpions and centipedes were plentiful, the ants were the worst of it.

---

[1] THESE ANTS, WHICH ALMOST CERTAINLY BELONG TO THE GENUS *DORYLUS*, HAVE BEEN CALLED THE HUNS AND TARTARS OF THE INSECT WORLD. THEY ARE CERTAINLY AMONG THE MOST AMAZING OF GOD'S CREATURES. I MUST CONFESS, AFTER HAVING BEEN DRIVEN FROM MY BED BY THEM IN THE MIDDLE OF THE NIGHT, SEVERAL TIMES IN INDO-CHINA, THAT, HATE THEM AS I DID, I WAS NONE THE LESS FORCED TO RESPECT THEIR ARMIES. WHEELER SAYS THAT "THEIR VAST ARMIES OF BLIND, BUT EXQUISITELY COOPERATING WORKERS, FILLED WITH AN INSATIABLE, CARNIVOROUS APPETITE, AND A LONGING FOR PERENNIAL MIGRATIONS, ACCOMPANIED BY A MOTLEY HOST OF CAMPFOLLOWERS, ALL SUGGESTS TO THE OBSERVER WHO FIRST COMES UPON THESE INSECTS IN SOME TROPICAL THICKET, THE EXISTENCE OF A SUBTLE, RESISTLESS AND UNCANNY AGENCY, DIRECTING AND PERMEATING ALL THEIR ACTIVITIES." AND AGAIN, WHEELER WRITES, "ALL SPECIES OF *DORYLUS*, SOME TWO DOZEN IN NUMBER, ARE CONFINED TO AFRICA, SOUTHERN ASIA, AND THE ADJACENT LARGER ISLANDS. THE WORKERS ARE COMPLETELY BLIND WITHOUT VESTIGES OF EYES, AND VARY GREATLY IN SIZE IN THE SAME COLONY, FROM LARGE SOLDIERS WITH TOOTHED MANDIBLES AND EXCISED CLYPEUS, THROUGH INTERMEDIATES, TO SMALL WORKERS WITH SMALL HEADS AND MANDIBLES. THE FEMALES ARE HUGE, UNWIELDY CREATURES, BLIND AND WINGLESS LIKE THE WORKERS, AND WITH A PECULIAR PYGIDIUM AND AN ENORMOUS GASTER, TO ACCOMMODATE THE VOLUMINOUS OVARIES. THE MALES ARE ALSO VERY LARGE, WITH GREAT EYES AND OCELLI AND SICKLE-SHAPED MANDIBLES . . . PARTICLE BY PARTICLE IS CARRIED OUT BY THE STEADY STREAM OF SMALL WORKERS, AND THE SOLDIERS, LARGE AND SMALL, WATCH ON BOTH SIDES OF THE LINE, EVER READY TO ATTACK ANYTHING THAT MAY APPROACH. THEY ASSUME A VERY PECULIAR ATTITUDE, WITH MANDIBLES WIDE OPEN AND THE HEAD AND THORAX BENT UPWARD AND BACK, UNTIL IT FORMS A RIGHT ANGLE WITH THE ABDOMEN. WHEN THEY SEIZE ANYTHING, THE ABDOMEN CAN BE TORN OFF WITHOUT THEIR LOOSENING THEIR GRIP. THEY ARE GREATLY FEARED BY THE NATIVES, AND EVEN THE GREATEST LAGGARD MOVES RAPIDLY WHEN PASSING THE 'LINE.'

"They even drop on one from the trees," she wrote, "and sting until one has stripped off every stitch in a frenzy. This does not take long, however, as all I wear when not hunting is a pair of blue pyjamas, made like a Chinese suit, and sneakers. It is a delicious outfit, and most satisfactory for both day and night wear. All that is necessary on arising is a dip in the sea, which is quite safe if one stays in where the waves break.

"We get up with the daylight, and go to bed with the dark, while the bonfires flicker through the leaves of our huts, and the surf pounds up in a line of white foam. The sky is brilliant, with the mountains silhouetted black against it, and the Southern Cross rides high above our heads. It is a crime to think how few of us ever cross the Equator into this hemisphere. We run from end to end of our northern half, yet seldom pass the line into this so different and beautiful part of the world. It all seems very small when one is half way round it and can reach home in five short weeks.

"In the morning the cockatoos wake us with the first streak of light, and we dress in the dark, in order to get started before the heat of the day. After visiting the baits with camera and gun, we return for a swim and lunch, about twelve. Then a snack of sleep, and off again for fishing or hunting until dark.

"Late this afternoon, D. and I went to get some birds for supper. We could hear a hundred different calls coming from every tree, but could see nothing except an occasional flash of orange or blue wings. Then, as the sun went down, they began flying everywhere through the golden light. This is by far the most beautiful time of day, and when the shadows of evening begin creeping over the land, I cannot describe the still sweetness of the air, the marvelous colors reflected from the sky, or the many fascinating sounds that steal up the mountainsides as the darkness gathers. As we walked up the beach toward home, Douglas shot two ducks, practically by moonlight. We could hear the wild pigs grunting around us, and our camp-fires shone ahead, on the circle of huts and the naked bodies of the natives. Then came a supper of soup, toast, roast pig, fried potatoes, carrots, rice cakes with syrup, and coffee; so you see, we fare regally. After this, the guns are cleaned, plans laid for the morrow, and bed feels very good, with two warm blankets to cover one."

By this time we had found cobras, pit-vipers, true vipers, and back-fanged snakes, all abundant. Komodo, therefore, unlike any other part of the world except India, is cursed with all four classes of poisonous snakes.

The true viper we had found was Russell's viper, the home of which is India, and, as they have hitherto been unknown in eastern Malaysia, the finding of one on Komodo was as fancy as anything we could have hoped for. It is curious and extremely difficult to account for this great gap in distribution, the long jump, as it were, between the little island of Komodo and India, a jump of some thousands of miles. Moreover, as the Komodo viper is the identical species that appears in India, it would seem certain that at one time it must necessarily have extended over the entire intervening area, and that its range, so to speak, was subsequently reduced. Here, again, we come up against an interesting problem. What conditions have favored its survival on Komodo? What has caused its extinction throughout the rest of Malaysia?

Several of the species of poisonous snakes which give so much trouble in India, where between 20,000 and 25,000 deaths occur annually due to ophidic accidents, were well represented on Komodo. It behooved us, therefore, to be extremely careful, especially as we had nothing but a general serum, which would, I fear, have proved quite inadequate. The demand for

102

Mrs. B and Lee Fai at base camp, Komodo. The roof of woven leaves harbored all manner of beasts, including pit-vipers, lizards, centipedes, spiders, etc. Indeed a most interesting collection could have been made from our shelter.

snake serum is constantly increasing, and for that reason the effect of different venoms has been observed very accurately.

Amaral points out that the composition of the poisons of different species of snakes is variable, the toxic quality depending largely on the food of the species. That is, the venom of the water-moccasin, which is piscivorous, is very active to fish; that of *Micrurus* (*Elaps*), which is ophiophagous, is very active toward other snakes; while that of *Bothrops insularis*, a tree living avivorous species, has an instantaneous effect on birds. Those poisons, therefore, whose toxic effect is particularly adapted to cause immediate death to certain animals, has a variable effect on man.[2]

---

[2] LET US TAKE AN EXAMPLE FROM EACH OF THREE CLASSES OF POISONOUS SNAKES, AND NOTE THE EFFECT OF THEIR POISON ON MAN.

I QUOTE FROM AMARAL. FIRST OF ALL, I WILL SELECT NAJA NAJA, A COBRA, COMMON IN INDIA, MALAYSIA, AND VERY ABUNDANT ON KOMODO. THE SPECIAL SYMPTOMS CREATED BY ITS BITE ARE AS FOLLOWS:

"THE VENOM PRODUCES AN INTENSE LOCAL BURNING SENSATION, EDEMA AND CONGESTION; COLD SWEATS; ACCELERATED AND THREAD-LIKE PULSE; RAPID RESPIRATION AT FIRST, WHICH LATER BECOMES WEAKER AND SLOWER. DIFFICULTY OF SPEECH OCCURS; MUSCULAR PARALYSIS PROGRESSES BY DEGREES; AND SOMETIMES HEMORRHAGES OCCUR THROUGH THE MUCOSA. IF THE DOSE OF POISON IS NOT SUFFICIENT TO CAUSE ACCENTUATED PARALYSIS, THE PATIENT WILL RECOVER, AND THE GENERAL SYMPTOMS WILL DISAPPEAR RAPIDLY. IF THE CONTRARY HAS OCCURRED, THE PATIENT DIES FROM RESPIRATORY PARALYSIS, THE HEART ACTION CONTINUING A SHORT TIME."

RUSSELL'S VIPER (VIPERA RUSSELLII), AS HAS BEEN STATED, BELONGS TO THE CLASS OF TRUE VIPERS. THE CHARACTERISTIC EFFECTS OF ITS VENOM ARE A "STRONG LOCAL REACTION, DEVELOPING ECCHYMOSIS, AND HEMORRHAGES. THERE ARE ALSO ACCENTUATED GENERAL PHENOMENA, CONSISTING PRINCIPALLY OF A TENDENCY TO COLLAPSE, RAPID AND THREAD-LIKE PULSE, NAUSEA, VOMITING, PUPILLARY DILATION, AND LOSS OF CONSCIOUSNESS. IF THE PATIENT RESISTS IMMEDIATE DEATH, THE LOCAL EDEMA SPREADS RAPIDLY; THERE ARE HEMORRHAGES AT THE POINT OF THE BITE, OR INTO THE MUCOUS MEMBRANES; HEMATURIA AND ALBUMINURIA OCCUR, AND FINALLY ANEMIA AND INTENSE EMACIATION, CAUSING DEATH."

TRIMERESURUS FLAVOVIRIDIS, AN EASTERN SPECIES OF PIT-VIPER, PRODUCES A POISONOUS EFFECT COMPARABLE TO THAT OF THE PIT-VIPERS OF KOMODO, OR THE DREADED FER-DE-LANCE OF CENTRAL AND SOUTH AMERICA.

"FORMIDABLE REACTION OCCURS—THE PAINS ARE TERRIBLE." "LATER,' THERE ARE GENERAL SYMPTOMS, CONSISTING OF PARCHED THROAT, THIRST AND CONGESTION. FINALLY THE PATIENT BECOMES COMPLETELY EXHAUSTED, THE BODILY TEMPERATURE FALLS, AND DEATH OCCURS."

IT IS EVIDENT FROM THE ABOVE THAT, ALTHOUGH IN THE CASE OF THE COBRA AND THE PIT-VIPER, THERE IS A CHANCE OF RECOVERY, THE BITE OF RUSSELL'S VIPER WOULD BE FATAL, FOR, EVEN IF THE PATIENT RESISTS IMMEDIATE DEATH, ANEMIA AND INTENSE EMACIATION SET IN, BRINGING DEATH SOMETIMES A WEEK LATER.)

Under Defosse's direction, the coolies meanwhile, had been constructing leafy screens, or "bomas" near the baits, from which we could observe the lizards, and shoot such specimens as appeared to be desirable for our museum groups. The coolies were very wary of *Varanus komodoensis*. Doubtless, *V. k.* would have served the purpose of their midnight orgies more effectively than *Varanus salvator*—a species common throughout Malaysia. The Singhalese, however, put *salvator* to a different purpose. According to Sir J. G. Tennent, "the skillfulness of the Singhalese in their preparation of poisons and their addiction to using them are unfortunately notorious traits in the character of the rural population. Among these preparations, the one which above all others excites the utmost dread, from the number of murders attributed to this agency, is the potent kabara-tel, a term which Europeans sometimes corrupt into cobra-tel, implying that the venom is obtained from the hooded snake; whereas, it professes to be extracted from the Kabara-goya (*Varanus salvator*).

"In the preparation of this mysterious compound, the unfortunate Kabara-goya is forced to take a painfully prominent part. The ingredients are extracted from the heads of venomous snakes by making incisions in the heads of these reptiles, and suspending them over a basin to collect the poison as it flows. To this, arsenic and other drugs are added, and the whole is boiled in a human skull, with the aid of three Kabara-goyas, which are tied on three sides of the fire, with their heads directed towards it, and tormented with whips, to make them hiss, so that the fire may blaze. The froth from their lips is then added to the boiling mixture, and, as soon as an oily scum rises to the surface, the kabara-tel is complete. Before commencing the operation of preparing the poison, a cock has to be sacrificed to the demons.

"The ugly lizard is itself regarded with such aversion by the Singhalese that if one enter a house or walk over the roof, it is regarded as an omen of ill-fortune, sickness or death; and, in order to avert the evil, a priest is employed to go through a rhythmical incantation."

Salvator, when compared with the Komodo lizards, hardly excites remark. If a Singhalese priest has to undertake rhythmical incantation to avert the evil eye of *salvator*, what would he not have to do, if *komodoensis* stepped into his front door?

So far, we had killed five of the big lizards—the largest a little more than nine feet. Many more, however, had been caught alive in the spring traps built by Defosse. A strong tree is bent over and fastened down. The release is cunningly contrived so that when the lizard puts his head through the noose, to reach the bait, he receives the surprise of his life by being jerked aloft. Coolies then run out of the jungle and lasso the infuriated animal, who very soon finds himself lashed to a strong pole, unable to move.

For hours at a time, we watched the beasts as they devoured the bait. Voracious as they are, it was interesting to note what a careful lookout they kept, especially the smaller ones, who seemed terrified when an adult made his appearance. When a small lizard turned and dashed away with lightning speed, it was an almost certain indication that a large one was approaching. For several minutes the observer in the boma might see absolutely nothing, and then suddenly, from behind a tree, a big black head with two dark beady eyes would appear and remain entirely motionless, while the eagle eyes, sunken grimly beneath projecting supraorbital bones, would survey every inch of the ground, ready to detect the slightest move. When the beast was assured that all was well, he would lower his head, flash a long yellow bifurcated tongue into the air, and then move rapidly toward the bait as if ready to bolt the

This spot which portrays at once the most beautiful and characteristic features of Komodo was selected for the background in the American Museum group.

whole carcass with one greedy gulp. The impression he gave as he came ponderously forward was one of great weight and strength. Indeed, although the small ones looked rather slim and agile, the adults are thick-set, muscular creatures, with a very heavy body. After a length of seven feet is attained, the weight increases, so that at between seven and eight feet it is, I believe, doubled. This accounts, no doubt, for the erroneous stories regarding the lizard's measurements.

In the process of gorging himself, the long sharp claws are used indiscriminately to scrape and tear with, while the thin, recurved teeth with serrated edges are employed to rip off great chunks of the foul meat. The beast maneuvers this by seesawing back and forth on braced legs, giving a wrench at the bait with every backward move. Sometimes, in this position with jaws buried deep in the meat, and neck curved forward and down, he resembles nothing so much as paintings of Tyrannosaurus, restored. When a piece of flesh has been detached, he lifts his head and gulps down the whole slab, regardless of size. As the food goes down, the skin of the neck becomes distended in the most astonishing fashion. Then he licks his chops, rubs both sides of his face on the ground, as if to clean it, and lifts his head, the better to observe the landscape. On one occasion, a lizard swallowed the whole hind quarters of a boar at one gulp—hoofs, legs, hams, vertebrae and all. If he is surprised when so engaged the results are apt to be disastrous, for this beast is easily excited, and immediately disgorges himself. The feeding process is loathsome to watch, and I have even seen the lizards run off with strips of intestines dangling from their jaws.

One of the most characteristic positions of *Varanus komodoensis* is taken when he is scanning his surroundings with his head aloft. His hind quarters and tail are on the ground, while his forelegs are braced, his head reaching into the air. In this position he will remain motionless for many minutes, and, occasionally, if he desires a still better view, he will sit up on his haunches, with fore-feet dangling like those of a rabbit. This attitude is only rarely assumed but, sitting thus, the animal is most impressive.

In the boma, no precaution need be taken about noise, for these diurnal animals are quite deaf. Many times we have shouted noisily without the slightest effect. Unfortunately, we were able to find none of the eggs, nor any clew as to where they might be found.

One evening we released five *varanae* on the beach as a test, for we wished to determine their swimming ability. Also, we wanted to know whether or not they would take to the sea of their own free will—an important question with regard to their restricted distribution. Of five lizards let loose, one large and one small one immediately fled to the sea, without the slightest hesitation. Two others headed for the jungle, while a fifth ran down the beach for 150 yards, went up into the grass, and then deliberately walked down to the water's edge, and proceeded to swim far out into the bay. The largest one which had taken to the water immediately submerged for a full two minutes, and then reappeared a hundred yards away, swam down the beach for half a mile, and ambled slowly off into the jungle. When swimming, their heads are carried well above the surface of the water, so that they can be seen at a great distance, but on the whole these lizards cannot be said to be good swimmers, their movements being rather clumsy and ineffective.

We used deer and boar to bait our traps, and, so plentiful are these animals on Komodo that hunting them is not the sport it might be. One evening I stalked a wild boar for about half an hour, and finally met him head on in thick jungle at about twenty yards, and killed him. We were in need of four more for bait, so I continued hunting and at last, when it was almost dark, discovered a whole herd of them rooting out among the rocks on the beach at low tide. Of these, it was almost too easy to kill the four I needed.

About this time, Dr. Dunn killed another cobra, and might well have attempted to catch it in his hands, had not Defosse been there to prevent him. As Dr. Dunn is a herpetologist, and therefore knew a hundred times as much about reptiles as Defosse, it may seem curious that it was the latter who put out the restraining hand. However, the truth is, that although Dunn had doubtless handled hundreds of dead cobras in a laboratory, yet Defosse, who was accustomed to see them in the field, could recognize one at a distance much more quickly.

Having made as many studies of the lizards as it was possible to do from our camp on the beach, we decided to move up to the spot I had found high on the mountain ridge, in the center of the island. Defosse started ahead with the natives to get the camp ready while B. and I walked down the beach and took a farewell look around the village of Komodo, the only inhabited point on the island. It is an altogether wretched place, full of mangy dogs and sickly children, consumption and venereal disease. With abundant game at hand, these people yet make no attempt to vary their fare, preferring to grub around the coral reefs, collecting sea-food. A sorry spectacle they presented. It is depressing to see humanity when it reaches such a degraded state.

Before leaving for the mountains, we transferred two captured lizards to a new and stronger cage, and we had quite an exciting time doing it. With the cages set end to end, and the doors open in be tween, we first attempted to make the animals move by prodding them, but this was of no avail. Finally, we tied some dried grass to the end of a long stick, set fire to

On the lookout! Notice muscles in shoulder.

He breaks the manila rope that holds the bait and carries the whole boar away.

FROM THE MOTION PICTURE

Varanus komodoensis as he is often seen prowling over the rugged mountains of Komodo.

Lizard walking quickly through grass.
FROM THE MOTION PICTURE

112

Feasting.

He has the whole boar in his mouth. Notice tail of bait under lizard's neck.

FROM THE MOTION PICTURE

it, and inserted it at one end. This at last had the desired effect, and, one after the other, their red mouths open, their jaws
drooling a villainous slime, they rattled into their new cage,
hissing horribly, lashing their tails and scratching so violently
that their claws came off. Such was the general excitement that
one vomited up the whole leg of a pig, which, incidentally, was
later re-eaten with gusto.

The next day, poor B. had to face the agony of a terrible
climb. "It was a nightmare," she wrote, "with the stones rolling from under foot at every step, your eyes blinded with the
sweat that poured into them, and the sound of your heart roaring and pounding in your ears, like a cataract." However, on
finally topping the last rise of ground, the sight that greeted
our eyes was pleasing beyond words. Imagine a large basin of
rolling, park-like country, dotted here and there with patches
of jungle and palm trees. Imagine on the floor of the basin a
circle of palm huts, open at both ends to the cooling breeze.
Then scatter a few natives among the huts, hang a dead buck in
the shade of a mimosa tree, let the wind ripple across the mellow fields of grass and paint a few puffy white clouds against a
hard, azure sky, and you have the picture.

Never did camp look more alluring. Shortly after our arrival, Chu served us with a civilized meal in his usual surprising fashion. It is always so with good Chinese servants; things
happen as if by magic, and the resulting concoctions are delicious. In the evening B. took a bath in our rocky pool.

Thus, by the time she had revelled in a supper of fresh
venison by the light of the full moon, she had entirely recov-
ered her usual excellent spirits. Poor Lee Fai, however, dragged
his delicate carcass into camp hours after the rest of us had
arrived. He simply babbled the same sentence over and over
again: "Walking much trouble! Walking much trouble!" And
then good-natured old Chinaman that he was, he burst out

Mrs. Burden with one of the smaller lizards that she shot.

laughing. The poor boy cut a pathetic figure, for he simply did not "savvy." Even after all this time, he did not dare venture forth from camp unescorted, for he was still convinced that tigers lurked in those jungles.

Defosse and I meantime had been off exploring. There were fresh buffalo tracks everywhere, so that we were very wary of every thick clump of bamboo. If you pass too close, these great beasts are apt to surprise you with a charge that leaves little opportunity for escape. On our way up to the divide, we saw innumerable deer and wild boar, and pigeons of every variety, whose booming voices resounded through the jungle. This was an ideal country to hunt over, the uneven terrain making stalking an easy matter. As we reached the backbone of the island, a big buck sprang up in front and coughed at us, a strange, miserable sound for so beautiful a creature. From the crest we could look down on all sides, to a sunlit sea dotted here and there with islands of indescribable shape, that stood out black against the silver of wind-swept water. The sun was setting, and with its setting, the western sea glowed with the blood-red embers of the dying day. To us, standing there on the mountain top, the island beneath our feet seemed like a great ship sailing a painted sea.

Then we saw *Varanus* tracks, and a great hole in the hillside, under a massive boulder, in front of which was a level spot. Here, obviously, the beast disported himself, and basked in the sunshine.

And then, when the mist crept up the thickly wooded gulches, and the moon swam up above the palm trees, we fell to talking, the old hunter and I. "One might take many walks in many countries of the world," he said, "and not have one half as interesting as this has been. I would like to bring my whole family and settle here, and be King of Komodo."

When I returned to camp, everyone had gone to sleep,

116

This monster swallowed the entire hindquarters of a deer at one gulp.

save two natives who were playing their bamboo flutes by the campfire, yonder. There was the glisten of a white moon on wet grass, and the murmur of small voices from out of the leafy darkness of the jungle. I could hear the gentle rustle of a sleepy forest talking to itself. Never was night more enchanting! There was the rattle of green bamboo, the rich fragrance of the "orchid-scented glade," and a pleasurable feeling of how little importance here is man. "The spirit of place" as sighing on the night wind, with every breath of air that stroked those ancient hills. Now there was a ghostly murmur reminiscent of aeolian music in a pine forest. What magic the moon makes, and how inexpressibly subtle the charm of such a scene!

Tracks of a large Varanus in the mud. In the millions of years to come such tracks as these may well be the fossil imprints of an extinct species. Note the mark of the tail between the tracks.

CHAPTER VII

TO BE THE KING
OF KOMODO

We were still putting out baits, and for that reason I killed a boar early one afternoon and built the necessary blind. After that I happened to run onto a water-buffalo—a solitary bull lying down at the edge of some thick bamboo jungle. This time, I was prepared to attack him, for I was armed with steel bullets. But I was destined to come off badly a second time in an encounter with the wild buffalo. And perhaps it is well to describe an incident in which the hunter is forced to retire with all speed: such incidents are usually omitted.

The Komodo buffalo are descendants of tame buffalo gone wild, and therefore differ somewhat from those that have never suffered from the yoke of man. The true wild buffalo will never venture into the jungle. The open plains are their home. The descendants of buffalo that have gone wild, however, always live in the cover of the jungle, coming out to feed only at night. Nevertheless, when they are attacked, the old instinct is dominant, and they prefer to stand their ground in the open, just as their wild brothers do. In this particular case, the solitary bull was, as I have said, right on the edge of the jungle, and, despite instinct, I did not see how he could resist jumping into cover if attacked from the open side. Such was the lay of the land and the direction of the wind that I found it quite impossible to get closer than 250 yards without running the risk of being seen or winded. This was probably very fortunate for me, for, although I did not have the slightest suspicion of it at the time, the barrel of my rifle had begun to give out, and as the bullets no longer fitted tight, they were dropping two or three feet in a hundred yards.

At last, taking the greatest possible care, I fired. Immediately the bull strode defiantly right out into the open sunlight, and there stood with legs far apart and head thrown back, a spectacle of dauntless courage. Due to the angle at which the sun struck his body, the gigantic muscles of his neck and shoulders stood out in beautiful relief, so that he gave the impression of tremendous power. He made a fine target, and I continued firing, wondering the while why I could not bring him down. Now and then he tossed his head into the air, shook his great horns, pounded his heavy fore hoofs on the ground, and whirled this way and that with sudden vicious movements, as if searching for the source of danger. Any hunter would be proud to bag such a magnificent beast.

I realized quite well that he was looking for trouble, and that if he located me he would probably charge at once, which was not very comforting in view of my ineffective shots. So he stood his ground valiantly, while I—hiding behind some blades of saw-grass—shot off my last steel cartridge.

Just at this moment, the old bull must have concluded that he had been peppered at long enough, for, although I am certain that he had not seen me, he started on a full gallop towards me. For a few moments I stayed where I was, watching the great thundering beast rolling towards me like a locomotive, a cloud of dust rising in his wake. Then, jumping up, I ran. Getting a little knoll of ground between myself and the bull, I turned and looked once more. He was still coming at top speed, head up, and apparently quite unharmed. At last I made up my mind to join the coolies, who were already in headlong flight. Yes, I even intended to pass them; once you have determined upon a policy of flight, there can be no object in loitering. Moreover there is a certain amount of fun and excitement, a certain thrill, in running away, when you know that nothing can be gained by holding your ground. As a result, although the bull did not follow us far, I fairly dove to safety in the jungle, and enjoyed a rather nervous but hearty laugh at my ignominious retreat.

So ended my second unsuccessful encounter with a solitary bull. Late in the evening I went with Defosse, and we killed a young bull, but it was a rather ordinary, uneventful stalk.

Meantime, the poor little Lee Fai had missed some marvelous opportunities to get moving pictures of deer and buffalo, but really it was not his fault, for he was quite blind—a serious handicap for the photographer of wild life.

As for B., her nerves were on edge that evening, which is natural, when you consider that she and Dunn had been watching at a blind all afternoon, and had heard buffalo close by in the jungle. As they were not equipped with steel bullets, they crawled up onto a big rock.

> "I cannot describe the relief afforded by this maneuver," she wrote. "I have since discovered that the crashings were not imaginary, but a whole herd of wild buffalo. In the future I shall not be seen much on terra firma. My condition is such that I am not happy unless perched on rocks or trees. Even then, I imagine cobras slithering down my back. It is great to be the wife of a naturalist. Every woman should try it once, to prove her love for her husband. It is the best test I can think of, especially as it is essential to keep in the spirit of the thing, and learn to

A twelve inch centipede.

A cobra—Naja naja sputatrix.

love every goddam one of God's creatures! What courage, merely to laugh shrilly when a centipede emerges from one's trousers, when roaches build their nests in one's boots, and the ticklings of thousands of legs denotes the presence of ants, spiders, beetles, ticks and fleas, by day and by night! Even the food, cold cream, and tooth paste are filled with the former of these pests. So far, we have discovered only three scorpions in our bedding, but, of course, in my dreams they are always there."

Speaking of centipedes and scorpions, those on Komodo are certainly among the largest in the world. Size, however, in the insect world is no criterion. A small species of centipede may be more poisonous than a large one; but it is not likely. Of course, I could get no idea from the natives how dangerous it was to be bitten by one of these twelve-inch "hundred-feety," and as I did not propose to test it out myself, I could not get any accurate information on the subject.[1]

Beyond the rolling open country which surrounded our camp was a big black wood that swept up the steep mountain slopes and merged with the cloud forest above. On entering it, Dr. Dunn saw in the space of a few yards, a black cobra, a centipede of enormous proportions, a scorpion, bats and other horrible creatures that are altogether attractive to a zoologist. Defosse disliked the place and called it the Prehistoric Wood; he cared little about venturing into its depths. Dunn prowled around in it for hours on end, lost himself, had a wonderful time, and finally emerged with a smile of glee and a various assortment of venomous creatures which were exhibited in turn to all and then immersed in formaline.

As for B. and myself, we were inquisitive and liked to satisfy our curiosity, but it was quickly satiated, and when we emerged from the wood, it was with a feeling of shaking off something very unpleasant in which we had been entangled.

We had both just been in the very womb of this forest—a place where great blocks of porous lava are strewn prodigiously in every direction, and deep bat filled caves excite one's wonder. Everywhere there were coiling vines and contorted creepers that dangle through mid-air from the green canopy above. Giant hawsers, twisted, gnarled and knotted, ugly in shape, hung suspended overhead. Giant lianas encircled the most beautiful trees in a viselike embrace, causing strangulation. Epiphytic plants sprouted from every limb. In all the aisles of the jungle grew superb specimens of the banyan, from the sweeping branches of which cables plunged to the ground. These take root, feed and support the branch, so that in turn it can drop new stems to earth and raise new branches in the air. On all sides were inextricable tangles of knotted, musty and undulating roots which crawled over the earth till they united and rose in the form of a flying buttress, thus to support some monarch of the jungle.

B. and I plunged through this place of gloom where death lurks in every byway, and at last following a buffalo trail, we emerged at one step from dismal solitudes into the light of day. It was a relief to get out of that musty, stifling forest, and to stand in the open sunlight once more with the wind in our faces and the waving grass about our feet, the bay below us and a view "far over the summer sea," of mountains rising one above the other into the hazy distance.

We had been standing there but a few minutes enjoying the incomparable view, when of a sudden a big black *Varanus* emerged from the Prehistoric Wood, to our left. At the same moment a wild boar trotted out in his direction from an isolated clump of bamboo in front of us. Now, at last, thought I to myself, we may see something interesting, which will prove definitely whether or not *V. k.* dares to attack a full-grown boar. So we sank slowly into the grass, and I took out my field glasses, in order to watch it more closely. It is useless to describe every move of the two beasts, but the salient features are worth recording. In brief they are as follows:

The lizard was motionless on the edge of the jungle, watching the boar who trotted unsuspectingly toward him. The lizard (fearing, perhaps, that he might be seen by the boar) then slid silently into the jungle. At this moment, the boar caught the lizard's scent, and headed off toward a small patch of jungle at right angles to his former course. Presently the lizard reappeared, and, seeing no boar, wandered leisurely out across the open, stopping at frequent intervals to have a good look. About this time the pig emerged from his patch of jungle, saw the lizard headed away in the opposite direction, and, satisfied that his route was now clear, ambled along in his original course, stopping now and then to root. At this moment, the lizard might be said to have seen the boar out of the back of his head, for he suddenly turned, ducked, and headed back after the pig. Unfortunately, the pig saw him coming, and ran away into the Prehistoric Wood, and so the affair ended. No scientist could reach a verdict on such evidence. However, I do not believe for a minute that enough animals die a natural death on Komodo to supply thousands of *Varanus* with food. Therefore, as there are virtually no small mammals on the island, we are forced to the conclusion that they kill deer and pig for a living. I feel morally certain that this is true.

Moreover, my conclusion is verified by the Assistant Resident at Bima, who states that a large specimen of *Varanus komodoensis* had been taken alive on Komodo by certain Chinese poachers. This animal was brought to Bima and temporarily chained to a tree. While he was so chained, a small horse strolled by too close, whereupon the lizard jumped at the horse and took a great piece out of his side. When I asked to have the horse brought around in order that I might observe

PHOTO BY MRS. BURDEN

The author studying Malay at the 2000 foot camp on Komodo.

the marks, the Assistant Resident assured me that the unfortunate beast had been so severely wounded that it had to be shot. This story, which was corroborated by the Raja, I had no reason to doubt.

Just as B. and I were about to continue on our way, we were startled by Yiakut, our coolie, who at frequent intervals was emitting loud grunts. On turning to ascertain the cause of these weird exclamations, we found the man hunting gingerly under his sarong, as a monkey might hunt for a flea. Suddenly, he made a grab, and, with a series of gleeful grunts (for the Malay never shouts for joy) pulled a green tree-viper out along his bare skin from a fold of his garment, and held the venomous, wriggling thing suspended in the air. Exhibit A., I thought to myself. Only the day before, when Defosse and I were resting side by side in the grass, a very large cobra slipped right between us, and wriggled off down the mountain.

Meanwhile, the natives had seen a particularly ugly monster on the edge of the Prehistoric Wood, which they had excitedly described as the largest *boeja darat* (land crocodile) yet seen. He was a very wary fellow, so we decided that the best way to get him alive would be to build a trap at the edge of the forest, bait it with deer or pig, and then hide close by in a boma, ready to run out and lash him to a pole as soon as he was caught in the noose. Accordingly, Defosse killed an old razorback (wild boar) for bait, and the coolies set to work on the trap. Heavy stakes were pounded into the ground all around the bait, except for a large opening left at one end. The stakes were then lashed together with rattan, and the whole contraption carefully camouflaged with branches and leaves. A live tree was selected as the spring pole. The branches were cut, the rope tied to the top, and then, with all the combined strength of some fifteen coolies, the tree was bent over, and the noose set at the opening at the front of the trap. There was, however,

to be one difference between this set and all the others that
we had built hitherto. The small animals did not tempt us any
longer. We had trapped plenty already, and we did not want
the trap to spring when the small fellows came to feed on the
bait. It might spoil the whole show, for the wary old devil we
were after would probably be lurking in the immediate vicin-
ity in order to assure himself that all was well. The release was
therefore attached to a string that ran along the ground to the
boma. The trap could not go off until the string was pulled. In
this way, we could watch everything that went on and release
the spring pole at just the right second to send Mr. Dragon
whirling aloft among the branches. Then we could rush out
with our coolies and make him fast. The string leading to the
boma was well covered up with leaves and the boma itself thoroughly camouflaged. I tested it out several times. When the
string was pulled the tree swished upward, to my complete
satisfaction. Already, I visualized the great reptile dangling in
mid-air, struggling on the end of his tether. The whole contraption was Defosse's handiwork, and it was as pleasing to the
eye as to the imagination.

The next day we were on the job early in the morning,
for the bait had already begun to smell. For a long time we
waited in the boma, chatting together in leisurely fashion (for
it will be remembered that these animals are stone deaf) until a big reddish centipede crawled into our dark hiding place.
For a moment the excitement within the four walls of that
gloomy abode was intense. However, when one of the Malays
succeeded in deftly severing the beast in two with his machete,
or "parang," order was restored. After that, we did not feel
much like stretching out, and making ourselves comfortable,
and it was just as well that we didn't, for two scorpions presently made their appearance. These were dealt with after the
fashion of Malays, who either hold them over a hot ember till

they pop, or else cut off the stinger and then play with them as one would with a toy, their facial expression the while being a study in blanks.

By this time we were beginning to feel very uncomfortable in our congested quarters, but, as the sun was well up, it was time for the dragon lizards to be abroad, and accordingly we kept a close lookout. Presently a small *V.k.* appeared and maneuvered around and around the trap. He was followed very soon by a much larger beast (about the size of those that eventually reached the New York zoo), who immediately entered the trap and tried to drag the whole boar out. But the razorback had been carefully lashed in place, and could not be budged. Presently I saw him look up and then turn and flee into the jungle as if the very devil were after him. I told the men that I thought the big one was coming and to hold themselves ready. Then we waited without seeing or hearing a thing for about half an hour. Suddenly one of the coolies made a strange sound. Then he looked around at the other men, and seemed to be unduly excited. On peeping through the back of the boma, I saw that here, in truth, was a dragon—a living remnant of the monster lizards of the Pleistocene.

One black eye was fixed on the boma. I did not dare move. Now he started forward again. He was headed right for the boma. The coolie who had seen what was happening shrank back. I could see the ugly brute very well. He looked black as ink. His bony armor was scarred and blistered. His eyes, deep set in their sockets, looked out on the world from underneath overhanging brows. Defosse waited placidly without saying a word. Now the creature's footsteps were plainly audible. He passed right by on one side of the boma. I could have reached out and touched him with my hand, and I had the tingling sensation of actually having a dragon walk by within a yard of where I was standing. The coolies were very restless, and

The botanical gardens at Buitenzorg. Defosse and Dr. Dunn may be seen at right.

Defosse spent his time keeping them still.

After the beast had passed by the boma, there ensued one half hour of agony. He seemed to be very wary of a trap, and in a generally suspicious frame of mind. He would walk up to the opening, and almost put his head into the noose, but never quite far enough. Then he would inspect everything very closely, his snaky tongue in constant motion, and always, just as we expected him to take the fatal step, he would turn abruptly and walk away again, and sit motionless, looking into the surrounding jungle for five or ten minutes on end. This happened over and over again. My nerves were in a terrible state: I longed so to catch him that the suspense was almost unendurable.

Just at this moment I heard a vague hum in the distance. It grew louder and louder, and then, in a great roar, something seemed to be descending on our heads, as if an airplane were diving upon us with the engine full on. But it passed over us. The sound of millions of wings filled the air; a great swarm of bees passing low through the jungle. The sound died away again into a mysterious; hum barely audible, and after that I was conscious of a deathly silence save for a slight rustling of leaves overhead. The big lizard still remained immovable, as though fascinated by a sound he could not even hear. Then, all of a sudden, it happened.

He walked quickly up to the opening, stepped through the noose, and seized the bait. I jerked the release and it went off. The Dragon must have received the surprise of his life, for he found himself sailing into the air. At the same moment there was a terrible cracking, and as the beast, who had been literally thrown into the air, fell again, the rope tightened, and the spring pole cracked again and bent at the point of breakage, so that our prize, instead of being suspended in mid-air, was on the ground, tugging at the tether, which held him firmly about the middle. Then, as the coolies ran out to surround

Defosse (right) and the author discussing plans for capturing the dragon lizards alive.

him, the ugly brute began vomiting—a pleasant little parlor trick these creatures develop when excited. The Malays did not dare go within several yards of our captive, so now it was time for Defosse to get into action. He had been practising with the lasso for months past, and accordingly he stepped into the ring. A strange pair they made, the old hunter and his grim antagonist, who, by this time, was lashing himself into a frightful rage, the foam literally dripping from his jaws. But Defosse was wise. He was taking no unnecessary chances. The first throw missed, and he coiled his rope again as methodically as if he were practising on a tent peg in camp. The lizard was clawing frantically to get away. Defosse stepped up quite close behind him, while he was thus engaged in his struggles, and roped him about the neck. The end of the rope was made fast to a tree. A third rope about the tail, to prevent that weapon from doing damage, did the trick. There being no more danger, the Malays stepped bravely forward with their pole, hog-tied the unfortunate animal, lashed him to the pole, and started back to camp. The work was done and we were jubilant. Once in camp, we thrust him into the cage which we had especially built for him. As he was slowly introduced at one end of the oblong, box-like cage, the thongs that held him, one by one, were cut. When he felt himself free to move again within the four walls, he lashed himself into another magnificent fury. Then he began vomiting, and the smell was so appalling that we left him.

That night was another beautiful tropical night. The camp slept silently under the jungle moon, and meantime the dragon was getting to work. In the morning we found to our dismay that our prize catch had broken out and made good his escape. He was probably still making tracks for the other end of Komodo. This loss was the greatest disappointment of the entire expedition. We felt so sure of him that we hadn't even taken photographs. The wire that covered a large square air-hole at the top of his cage (the strongest wire, incidentally, that could be obtained in Batavia) had been ripped open. There was the hole gaping at us, as evidence of a degree of strength we had never suspected.

B. hunted as ardently as the rest of us. For hours on end she was watching at the baits. For days at a time she was scouring the mountains. On one occasion, after she had already shot several dragon lizards, she enjoyed a memorable experience. We had had breakfast as usual at the first streak of dawn. Before we had finished the meal, daylight rushed upon us, so that,

> "as Defosse and I started off," she wrote, "the sun was already gilding the tops of the great gubbong palms. The dew was still heavy under foot, and the myriad liquid sounds of the jungle were once more coming to life. One never becomes accustomed to the rosy wonder of a Malayan dawn, so sudden that the world is bathed in moonlight at one moment, and in sunlight the next. Just as sudden is the change in the temperature, so that, from shivering over our breakfast wrapped up in all our blankets, we shed everything like a cocoon with the coming of the sun, and start the day's hunting in the thinnest of clothes, never forgetting our helmets, which alone allow one to survive the terrible strength of the tropical sun.

> "As we neared the tree to which we had tied our dead deer, Defosse said to me, 'You must always be careful when passing these bamboo thickets, for the buffalo are liable to be resting in the shade during the day, and may charge out upon you.' No sooner had the words passed his lips than, with a terrific crashing and a bellow, a great black bull galloped from the side opposite us, and disappeared in the nearby jungle. 'Thank God for that!' he said, and we continued on our way, with legs that felt strangely like

jelly. This same hunter, by the way, was once caught by one of these animals and nearly gored to death. Unfortunately they are numerous on this island, though not so plentiful as the deer and wild boar that we see everywhere.

"Upon reaching the blind, we saw to our dismay that the bait had been torn completely in half, and the entire hind quarters devoured. Little did we suspect that one *Varanus* had been responsible for all this mischief, and, furthermore, that the whole half of a buck had been swallowed at one gulp. This we discovered later, but I must tell you how. My knees are still weak at the thought!

"As there was now no animal in sight, we went out to look for tracks around the bait. Defosse followed them down the hill on one side, while I looked round the other. Suddenly, something drew my attention to the edge of the jungle on my right, and there, sure enough, was one of our antediluvian monsters. For a moment, he stood partly concealed by the leafy jungle, and then, with heaving flanks and ponderous movements, he crawled forth into the light of day. At the same moment, I sank motionless into the tall grass, little realizing that I thus put myself directly in his path to the bait. "As he approached step by step, the great bulk of his body held clear of the ground, and the black beady eyes flashing in their deep sockets, I thought of the incredible beasts that moved through the shades of long ago. He seemed hardly to belong to this world—more fitting, I thought, that he should have crawled up from unthinkable solitudes of some bottomless gulch of the Inferno. A hoary customer, black as dead lava, whose very aspect spoke of indefinite existence, I wondered whither his ancestors had wandered on their endless journeyings to this enchanted isle.

"Occasionally, when he stopped and raised himself on those iron forelegs to look around, I could observe

Building the trap. One end of this box-like trap is left open. At this opening the noose is set. The natives are seen camouflaging the trap with leaves.

FROM THE MOTION PICTURE

Setting the trap. The trap now resembles a bush. The natives are bending the spring pole while Defosse at the entrance to the trap is setting the noose.

FROM THE MOTION PICTURE

the blistered battle-scars and indentations of his bony armor. Then, as he drew nearer, I suddenly realized my predicament. My gun was propped against the blind, where I had left it a few minutes earlier. Defosse was out of sight and the great reptile was continuing straight towards me. Should I jump up and run, thus losing the largest lizard we had seen in some time, or should I lie without moving, on the chance that Defosse would come back in time to shoot him, or that he would change his course and pass me unheeded?

"Nearer he came and nearer, this shaggy creature, with grim head swinging heavily from side to side. I remembered all the fantastic stories we had heard of these monsters attacking men and horses, and was in no wise reassured. Now listening to the short hissing that came like a gust of evil wind, and observing the action of that darting, snake-like tongue, that seemed to sense the very fear that held me, I was affected in a manner not easy to relate.

"The creature was less than five yards away, and that subtle reptilian smell was in my nostrils. Too late now to leap from hiding; he would surely spring upon me, rending me and serving my remains as he had served the dead deer. Better to take my chances where I lay, so I closed my eyes and waited.

"Then I opened them in time to see Defosse's head appearing over the hill. The next instant there was a flash, and a bullet buried itself in the great monster's neck. Like lightning he whirled and crashed toward the jungle, but once more the rifle did its work and he lay still!"

That night was our last delightful cold night in the mountains, for the next day we had to leave that earthly paradise and return to *The Dog*. Our camp was situated at nearly 2,000 feet altitude, and as the temperature falls at the rate of about

1°F per 300 feet altitude, it should have given us a difference of about seven degrees between there and sea level. This fact, however, does not account for or in any way accord with the night temperatures that we actually had there, which ranged between 50° and 60° F.

Our collections were now complete, and we were ready to move on. Of the *Varanus*, we took two live adult specimens, and twelve dead; that is, fourteen in all, or one less than the allowance of fifteen given us by the Governor General. All in all, we were well satisfied with the work, so we made our way back to Telok Sawa, where *The Dog* lay waiting for us at anchor.

I had sent Lee Fai down several days before to do some developing. On my arrival, I found the old gentleman in repose. That was characteristic. A bland smile pervaded his countenance. This, also, was characteristic. But when he suddenly got up and presented me with a box, saying, "All plate maka spoil," I could have killed him. The wretch had ruined my photographic plates in developing.

However, the damage was done, and there was no use worrying. B. and I were very hot, so we decided to take a swim off a coral island· nearby. The beaches of red sand slipped off into green water, where live coral grew. Beyond that, it dropped away into the deep blue of many fathoms. Thousands of fish swam in and out among the polyps. Now and then a large black fin sailed by over the still water. Then there was a commotion small fish jumped in every direction and the black fin disappeared. As we threw off our clothes and slipped into the sea, a reddish light slanted across the bay and struck the beach of red sand. Our little island was like a spot of fire in an ocean of greens and blues. We kept in close to the shore, diving among the beautiful growths of coral, of which the whole island was made. It was refreshing, cool, delicious. Then we noticed clouds of smoke issuing from the stack of *The Dog*. Our ship was getting under steam.

In a very short time we were sailing away from one of the most charming and romantic islands in the world. Already Komodo was far away, a great shadow that loomed up weird and indefinite in the distance, and it was not without deep regret that we left her lonely shores behind. Meanwhile, as night hurried lonely out of the East, and the flying fish darted here and there over the water like so many streaks of silver, *The Dog* stood out to sea briskly punching the waves on her way to the little known island of Wetar, which lies at the extreme eastern end of the Lesser Sunda Island chain.

[1] CURIOUSLY ENOUGH, IN THE STATE OF ARKANSAS LIVES A GENTLEMAN, W. J. BAERG, BY NAME, WHO HAS DEVOTED YEARS TO OBSERVING THE EFFECT OF INSECT BITES AND STINGS UPON HIS OWN PERSON. HE WRITES ME THAT THE FEW SCORPIONS AND CENTIPEDES HE HAS STUDIED ARE FROM THE SOUTHERN AND SOUTHWESTERN STATES AND THE REPUBLIC OF PANAMA, AND THAT HE CAN THEREFORE GIVE ME NO INFORMATION CONCERNING MALAYSIAN SPECIES. THE CENTIPEDES MR. BAERG HAS EXPERIMENTED WITH ARE SMALL—BUT A FEW INCHES IN LENGTH. LET US SEE THE EFFECT OF THEIR POISON.

"*SCOLOPENDRA POLYMORPHA* IS AN ACTIVE AND VIGOROUS CENTIPEDE FOUND IN CALIFORNIA.

"ON RATS. (8:10 A .M . SEPT. 17, 1923.) THE CENTIPEDE BIT AS SOON AS IT HAD BEEN CONVENIENTLY PLACED, AND, AFTER ABOUT FIVE SECONDS WAS REMOVED WITH CONSIDERABLE DIFFICULTY. THE RAT HELD THE LEG UP FOR A SHORT WHILE, THEN FAVORED IT WHILE WALKING. IT REMAINED QUITE ALERT, EYES WIDE OPEN AND TOOK SOME FOOD THAT WAS SUPPLIED. AFTER ABOUT THREE HOURS, (11 A.M.) THE RAT NO LONGER FAVORED THE LEG, AND APPEARED ENTIRELY NORMAL. THE PUNCTURES (ON THE INSIDE OF THE LEFT HIND LEG), WERE CLEARLY VISIBLE, BUT THERE WAS NO INFLAMMATION OR SWELLING.

"ON MAN. TWO DAYS LATER (7:45 A.M. SEPT. 19, 1923), THE SAME CENTIPEDE USED ABOVE WAS INDUCED TO BITE ME ON THE INSIDE OF THE TERMINAL JOINT OF THE SMALL FINGER. IT INSERTED ITS FANGS TWICE, AND THE SECOND TIME IT HELD ON SO TENACIOUSLY THAT I WAS OBLIGED TO LOOSEN IT WITH A PAIR OF FORCEPS. THE FANGS REMAINED INSERTED FOR 4-5 SECONDS. SMALL DROPS OF THE POISON, A CLEAR LIQUID, GATHERED OVER THE PUNCTURES. THE RESULTING PAIN WAS SHARP, LIKE THAT FOLLOWING THE PRICK OF A NEEDLE . IT WAS QUITE MARKED, BUT NOT SEVERE.) IT REMAINED NOTICEABLE, THOUGH GRADUALLY GROWING LESS, TILL IN A LITTLE OVER THREE HOURS, (10:55) IT HAD PRACTICALLY DISAPPEARED. NEAR THE PUNCTURES THERE APPEARED SMALL DROPS OF PERSPIRATION; THERE WAS NO DISTINCT REDDENING, NO CLEARLY VISIBLE WHITE AREA, NOR PERCEPTIBLE SWELLING."

THE SAME TYPE OF EXPERIMENTS HAVE BEEN MADE WITH SCORPIONS. TESTS MADE WITH THE SPECIES *VEJOVIS SPINIGERUS* OF SOUTHERN NEW MEXICO ARE AS FOLLOWS:

"ON RATS (8:10 A.M. SEPT. 22, 1923). THE SCORPION USED IN THE TEST STABBED THE RAT TWO OR THREE TIMES, AND APPARENTLY CAUSED CONSIDERABLE PAIN. WHEN PUT BACK IN THE CAGE, THE RAT LICKED THE INSIDE OF THE LEG RATHER VIGOROUSLY. IT WAS QUITE ALERT IN EVERY WAY AND APPEARED TO BE ENTIRELY NORMAL. IN WALKING IT DID NOT EVEN SEEM TO FAVOR THE LEG. OBSERVATION THROUGHOUT THE DAY FAILED TO SHOW ANY SYMPTOMS OF POISONING.

"ON MAN. A FEW DAYS LATER (8:00 A.M. SEPT. 25, 1923), THE SCORPION WAS ALLOWED TO

STING ME ON THE INSIDE OF THE SMALL FINGER OF THE LEFT HAND. IT STABBED QUICKLY TWO TIMES, SO THAT A BIT OF BLOOD GATHERED AT THE PUNCTURES. THE SENSATION WAS VERY MUCH LIKE THAT OF A PIN PRICK, AND THE RESULTING PAIN, WHICH WAS VERY SLIGHT, LASTED SCARCELY HALF AN HOUR. THERE WAS NO WHITE AREA AROUND THE PUNCTURES, AND NOT THE SLIGHTEST SWELLING OR INFLAMMATION."

MR. BAERG ALSO TRIED HIS EXPERIMENTS WITH TARANTULA, THE FAMOUS "BANANA SPIDER" OF THE CANAL ZONE, WHICH HAS THE REPUTATION OF BEING MORE DEADLY THAN A RATTLESNAKE. IN SPITE OF THE FACT THAT SEVERAL GUINEA PIGS HAD BEEN KILLED IN THE TEST, MR. BAERG YET HAD THE COURAGE TO EXPERIMENT ON HIMSELF.

"OR MAN. (8:44 A.M. AUGUST 29). IN THIS TEST, SOME PRECAUTIONS WERE TAKEN SO THAT I WOULD GET A RELATIVELY SMALL DOSE OF THE POISON. ONLY ONE FANG PUNCTURED THE SKIN, AND THIS WAS ALLOWED TO REMAIN FOR ABOUT ONE AND ONE HALF SECONDS. RATHER SEVERE PAIN DEVELOPED AT ONCE. IN A FEW MINUTES THE FINGER FELT NUMB AND THE PAIN WAS SO STRONG THAT I APPLIED DILUTE AMMONIA, ABOUT TEN SECONDS AFTER THE BITE HAD TAKEN PLACE. AT THIS TIME, THE SMALL FINGER WAS PERCEPTIBLY SWOLLEN, RATHER RED, AND STIFF. IN FIFTEEN MINUTES THERE WAS A STRONG THROBBING, AND THE SWELLING HAD INCREASED CONSIDERABLY. SOME MORE AMMONIA WAS APPLIED. IN THIRTY MINUTES THE FINGER WAS SO STIFF THAT IT COULD SCARCELY BE BENT, THE SKIN WAS VERY RED AND GLOWING, THE PAIN SEEMED SOMEWHAT LESS. IN AN HOUR THE SHARP PAIN HAD LARGELY SUBSIDED, THERE WAS A STRONG TINGLING SENSATION, AND THE STIFFNESS AND LAME FEELING EXTENDED TO THE THIRD FINGER. THE SWELLING GRADUALLY SPREAD OVER MOST OF THE HAND. IT DID NOT GO BEYOND THE WRIST.

"TWO HOURS AFTER THE BITE TOOK PLACE, (BELIEVING THAT THE EFFECT WOULD BE NO MORE THAN LOCAL) I DECIDED TO TRY HOT WATER AS A REMEDY FOR THE PAIN. AFTER KEEPING THE HAND IN COMFORTABLY HOT WATER FOR THIRTY MINUTES THE PAIN WAS PRACTICALLY GONE, MOST OF THE SWELLING HAD LIKEWISE DISAPPEARED, AND THE STIFFNESS WAS SOMEWHAT LESSENED. A PECULIAR SENSITIVENESS AND STINGING SENSATION, FELT WHEN GENTLY RUBBING THE SKIN, REMAINED FOR SOME TIME. ALL OTHER PAIN DISAPPEARED WITHIN SIX HOURS FOLLOWING THE BITE. A LAMENESS IN THE JOINTS OF THE SMALL FINGER PERSISTED FOR NEARLY A WEEK.

"*SERICOPELMA COMMUNIS* MAY, IN VIEW OF THESE OBSERVATIONS, BE REGARDED AS POISONOUS. THE EFFECT OF THE VENOM IS LIKELY TO BE SOMEWHAT PAINFUL, THOUGH PERHAPS IN MOST CASES NOT DANGEROUS."

CHAPTER VIII

THE SPLINTERED
MOUNTAINS OF WETAR

A little over four centuries ago, in 1504, Magellan sailed along the coast of Flores to Timor. It is impossible to realize that at that time everything between the East Indies and the Americas was unknown, and appeared as a vast blank on Behaim's new map of the world. I wonder in what light Magellan and his Captain, Vasco Da Gama, regarded these islands which were then separated by so many months and months of travel from home. No doubt it was while cruising here in the Banda Sea that the great navigator was inspired with the desire to chart the blank spaces on the map, and to circumnavigate the globe.

When Wetar sailed into our view one morning we were astonished, thrilled, and yet disappointed by what we saw. A more hostile-looking piece of country could not exist; the island should more properly be called Devil's Land. Wetar, in the first place, is entirely volcanic, and the volcanoes must have been of the explosive type, their heads having been shot off. The whole island is cut with ravines, gulches, and gorges, which seem to have splintered the mountains into a million jagged fragments. Due to the youthful stage of erosion and an arid climate, resulting in a rapid surface run-off, the cañons are deeply incised, with vertical walls. It is obviously impossible to effect a passage over them. However, one large stream has gouged a more open channel up which the traveler may force his way into the very heart of the melancholy mountains.

Here and there old lava flows end abruptly in walls several hundred feet high. Streams that were formed on the initial surface of these flows and once cascaded over the terminal cliffs, have now eaten out frightful gorges: within their forbidding recesses the light of day but dimly penetrates. An early morning sun casts such a jumble of jagged shadows that the whole landscape stands out in bold relief—a picture more arid and repulsive than the bad lands of the West. In the impersonal terms of science, we should say that the topography of Wetar is the result of immature erosion in an arid climate, on a series of steeply sloping lava flows, whose initial surface was quite irregular.

According to the sailing directions, the interior of Wetar is inhabited by fierce cannibal tribes belonging to the Papuan race. Several members of our expedition conceived from this literature such a desperate picture of ferocious tribes in their mountain fastnesses that they deemed it foolhardy to land. Our reception, however, at Kampong Oohok (native village on the north coast), dispelled all anxiety. Clad in their finest raiments, the population turned out en masse, and greeted us with flags, tomtoms, and bamboo flutes. The spectacle had elements of the ludicrous to western eyes, which made it difficult to preserve a gravity befitting the spirit of the occasion.

Missionaries have been at work in these seas, and the results of their labors have been made manifest. It so happened that on that beautiful July morning, a little naked savage was paddling lazily along the beach. On looking up, he chanced to see a great ship steaming in out of the blue. He ran back in terror to his Kam pong, and in a few minutes the whole village had gathered on the shore. Then, under orders of the headman, they dashed hectically back to their huts, to prepare themselves in what they chose to consider a more seemly attire. A few moments later they reappeared in Mother Hubbard gowns—raiments white as snow. Like a flock of self-conscious children, they now streamed down to the beach fully equipped to accord the great white masters a reception that be fitted their greatness. The spectacle, as I say, had elements of the ludicrous. When a savage attires himself in civilized dress and struts through his native village, he makes of himself a picture no less incongruous than would a naked aristocrat on Leicester Square.

Now, under the shifting glances of hundreds of wild eyes we rowed solemnly up to the beach. As the boat grated on the gravel shore there was a slight waver in the lines of white-uniformed Papuans, and the headman, accompanied by four braves holding a rickety stool above their heads, advanced towards us through the surf.

"I guess that settee is meant for you, B.," I called out.

"Good lord, do I dare!" she replied. "Look at the way they are holding it. They will surely drop me."

And so, in this magnificent style, with her arms clutching grizzled black necks, my wife was transported the entire ten feet that separated us from terra firma. We all fallowed in turn, until poor little Lee Fai rolled off at the crucial moment and fell sputtering into the water. This broke the spell, and the natives, after such a prolonged and unaccustomed restraint, enjoyed a hearty laugh at his expense. When quiet was restored and we had started a slow advance upon Kampong Oohok, the entire company clapped bamboo flutes to their lips and burst into song—but, instead of some barbaric, rhythmic tune, the hideous strains of "Yankee Doodle" (taught, no doubt, by the last mission aries) struck discordantly against our ears. It

The long yellow protrusible bifurcated tongue is used as a sensory organ.

is bad enough to hear it in New York, but to encounter it in the remote wilds of Wetar was monstrous. We were certainly doomed. The natives loved the tune, which is natural, when you consider that it was the only one they knew. They played it over and over and over again, following us as if in funeral procession, wherever we went. So it is, I thought, that savages serve their civilized guests. While interviewing the headman in his one-room hut, the music was temporarily suppressed at my special request. All the villagers then strained their ears to hear what words of wisdom the white lords would condescend to bestow. But when they discovered that the words of wisdom concerned the collecting of lizards and frogs, they seemed to be too dumbfounded even to view the matter as a jolly fine joke. That a group of white men should sail far across the sea to Wetar, and demand on their arrival lizards and frogs, was a matter even beyond conjecture.

Finally, after leaving full instructions concerning the collection of reptiles, we secured the necessary "jungly wallahs," (or coolies) and moved some six miles down the coast where we camped near the mouth of the river Lihoetaoe. We pitched camp at the very edge of the ocean, and, although sharks and crocodiles cruised daily up and down the shore, we took any pretext for a dip in the crystal water. No shelters of any kind were built, as we had decided to enjoy the great luxury of sleeping "à la belle étoile."

Every day or so, a Papuan family would paddle by in their out-rigger canoes, their pigs—which resembled the wild boar of Komodo—following them at a trot along the beach. Lee Fai was much puzzled by the action of these Wetar pigs.

"Never I see tings like dis before," he said, "pig for following behind man in jungle all same dog!"

B. took pleasure in keeping the camp supplied with fresh pigeon. They were so abundant that she could bring down any number with a rifle.

One night, her hunting brought her a more exciting experience. She and Defosse were following up a draw. Defosse, who was equipped with shotgun and bird shot, went first. B. heard something rustling ahead, off to the left. They made for it. At length, Defosse flashed two spots of light in the jungle. He guessed that they were either the eyes of a cuscus or a civet cat. The eyes moved away, and Defosse quickly followed into the underbrush. B. was left standing alone in the draw. A few minutes later, she heard Defosse fire. Immediately there was a terrific crashing, and the old hunter yelled, "Look out, it's a buffalo!" Being quite helpless, and in the dark, B. clung to a small tree, while the beast galloped blindly toward her. Finally, the hulking body came close, crashed by her, and thundered off into the jungle on the other side of the draw.

Defosse encountered the same wounded animal again the next evening, and not wanting to kill it, he had to take to the water so as not to risk a charge.

Collecting, meanwhile, progressed very satisfactorily. There is nothing very strange about collecting reptiles and amphibians. One simply wanders through the jungle, with eyes peeled alow and aloft. There goes a lizard scrambling up a tree trunk. A twenty-two pistol loaded with shot makes a mild report, and the dead lizard, after a superficial examination, is popped into a white cloth bag under the belt. Turning over stones and kicking rotting logs to pieces often yields good results. At night, with a light on one's head, one may follow up the dismal croakings of some tree frog for hours, without being able to locate the owner of the voice. On the other hand, if fortune favors, there may be an opportunity not only to observe the habits of some rare amphibian, but to record his actions by flashlight photographs taken at intervals. In this way, the life histories of these little creatures are worked out.

But to what end, the intelligent lay reader will ask, is all this collecting of frogs and lizards? To do the answer justice would require many pages. In short, it is as follows. Evolution, we now know, is a fact, and no longer a theory. We know also, something of how evolution takes place, but as to the why of evolution, absolutely nothing is known. The naturalist does not stop at the question How, he also asks Why, and, in order to answer this great question, every source of information must be probed. The birds of the Lesser Sunda Islands have been collected and studied. So, also, have the mammals. This explains, perhaps, why our expedition was of a herpetological nature. The problems of geology and zoögeography, of the relation of animal to environment, of survival and dispersal in this region where frequently the species is older than the island on which it is found, are too complex to allow of detailed analysis in these pages. Suffice it to say that collecting was proceeding apace, and that, having already obtained nine species new to the catalogue for Wetar, my attention turned to exploring.

One of my Papuan coolies, Maupelou, who had a certain meager knowledge of Malay, kept referring to the "Ayer besar" (the big water) up in the mountains. My curiosity having been aroused, I left B. in the care of Defosse, and started one day to find it. The enterprise brought dismay to Chu, who ran out as I left, and with touching anxiety in his voice, exclaimed, "Please Masta, I aflaid coolie man make beaty you !"

Maupelou had explained, with a few words of Malay, and many gestures, that if we left camp at sunrise, and traveled hard, we would reach the "Ayer besar" before noon. However, to be on the safe side, I took three days' provisions.

It was fortunate, too, that I did so, for at the end of a day's travel, we seemed to be no nearer the hidden lake. A few miles from camp we passed through Kampong Tara. While I was resting there, in the chief's hut, a withered looking old

A golden stream of sunlight and "Maupelou" in a canyon of Wetar.

scapegrace shuffled into view. "Good Lord!" I thought to my-self, "there's an old cannibal, if ever I saw one." White with skin disease, his teeth gone, his eyebrows arched meanly to-gether and his nostrils dilated, he stood there on splayed feet, with his long finger nails scratching among the folds of a tat-tered hide, so that scales of skin flaked off. He was as rascally an old savage as ever I hope to see. Aside from his headdress, earrings and other ornamentations, his only garment was a loin cloth wound around his waist. Quite different, I thought, must have been the bark girdle to which he had probably been accustomed in the bold days of his youth. This fierce old man of the forest, I felt, should be photographed. But when I in-vited him to pose before the camera, he remained perfectly dumb and immovable. Goodness only knows what was revolv-ing amid the obscure convolutions of his mind, as he sullenly frowned upon me, but I felt in my bones that it was something wholly unsavory. Some of the natives of the Kampong under-stood what I desired, and, having no superstitions with regard to the evil eye of the camera, eagerly prevailed upon the wretch to stand at the designated spot. With many explosions and low rumblings and mumblings, he eventually allowed himself to be pushed into the sunlight and I obtained my picture.

After leaving the village, our course took us up the river Lihoetaoe. From now on we were constantly wading and re-wading the rapids and slipping and falling on the rounded boulders. Maupelou and my other Papuan loped along briskly under their loads with an easy grace that proclaimed them to be real forest dwellers. On the other hand, the Malays, whom we had brought from Sumbawa, were forever lagging behind. We had here one more evidence of the relative superiority of the Papuans. Papuans are classed by anthropologists as "Oceanic Negroids," and yet, contrary to expectations, they are quick, bright, keen, full of smiles and laughter, very responsive and in no way afraid of hard work. The Malay, by contrast, is a dullard and a laggard; and as a forest dweller, he is but a poor imitation. Work is not a part of his philosophy; in his fight with the climate and vegetation of the tropics he has succumbed; now he lives simply as best he can off Nature's bounty. As a guide or companion in the jungle, I vastly prefer one Papuan such as Maupelou to any five Malays.

The term, Malay, is not very significant. According to Fay Cooper Cole, after a part of Malaysia had been inhabited by a people closely related to the Polynesians, they were joined by southern Mongoloids, who, for a long time, moved slowly southward out of the Peninsula of Indo-China. Pressure forced a marginal group of the Polynesians eastward. Those that remained behind became thoroughly mixed, thereby forming the Malay race. It is therefore evident that the chief difference between the Polynesian and the Malay is that the latter "possesses a greater amount of Mongoloid blood." Thus the Malay, in a sense, is a rather new arrival in the tropics, and has failed in many ways to master his surroundings. By heredity, he is essentially a man of the temperate zone. His stay in tropical climes can quite properly be viewed as a prolonged siesta, with emphasis on the siesta. The low class Malay is a lazy, indolent, happy-go-lucky, pleasant fellow, with little or no sense of humor, and a rather low order of intelligence. If he can avoid work, chew betel nut, keep a beautiful girl and a full belly, and otherwise be left alone, he considers himself blessed by the gods. Life has no more to offer. For the most part, the Malays are Mohammedans, but they are rather lax in their observances, fitting their religion to their wants as best they can.

The walls of the cañon up which we were traveling were constantly narrowing in, and by afternoon walking was becoming more and more arduous. We had been trudging along for some time in the jungle on the edge of the river, when suddenly we emerged, and I saw directly in front of me a Papuan maiden, stepping daintily through the water with a lithe grace that cannot possibly be described. Although very busy negotiating the rapid stream, she sensed my intrusion immediately, as any jungle creature would, and, uttering a little cry, turned around and started retracing her steps, meantime girding up her loins more tightly and deftly concealing a beautifully formed bosom from view. Maupelou then shouted to her in the dialect, no doubt assuring her that all was well. She looked shyly around from behind the great load of beeswax which she was carrying with a tumpline over her forehead, and hesitated for a moment while the water swirled around her well-turned limbs. I felt sure that I was the first white man she had ever seen. In order to look as harmless as possible, I sat down on a boulder and tried to watch her with an air of indifference and unconcern. At length, somewhat reassured, she came and stood beside me. A smile that was exquisitely subtle added beauty to her delicate features. So she stood, this wild, appealing little creature of the jungle, watching my every move as though ready to bound away at the slightest suspicion of danger. Her skin, quite different from the others I had seen, was of that warm golden hue which never loses its charm. Her face was beautifully moulded, her lips full, her hair wild, and her bewitching large round black eyes danced elusively from one to the other of us. They were liquid and lustrous and inquisitive as those of a doe, yet extremely intelligent. This untamed beauty laughed and chattered so that the musical sound of her voice tinkled through the forest, until it was time for us to resume the march again.

At the hour when the game begins to move again and the heat of the day has passed, we burst into a clearing of steaming hot springs. It was very unexpected and I found myself running eagerly back and forth from one to another of these fountains of boiling water. Hot springs are of interest to geologists

"As rascally an old savage as I ever hope to see."

chiefly as an indication of waning volcanic activity, while to the layman they excite admiration as one of the most beautiful of nature's wonders. Here I saw miniature mud volcanoes, perfect in their symmetry and form, with boiling water bubbling and hissing from the vent at the apex of the cone. Their sides were a marvelous network of greens and reds and yellows, shading one into the other. The multicolored terraces of silicious sinter were of dazzling beauty, especially when looking into the reflected sunlight. The steam swirls up from the vents like a filmy cloud. The spray glistens in the air, falls and then rolls like so many million tiny diamonds over the terraced steps. Alone in this deep valley of Wetar these springs bubble and hiss night and day, year after year, unadmired, their changing beauty wasted on the barren air, but from their very loneliness they hold a charm for the weary traveller inestimably greater than the famous geysers of the Yellowstone.

From here we passed on up the cañon into a jungle of giant trees, where the cuscus live and the little jungle people hunt for wax and honey. Then night swooped upon the forest and we camped.

The following day we continued our struggles with cañon, stream and forest until late in the afternoon, when I, for one, found myself too foot-sore and weary to proceed further. On either side of us the mountains swept up to giddy heights. Giant walls of naked rock hemmed us in. Shafts of sunlight plunged into the deep recesses like dagger thrusts. The stream, which had changed in character to a mountain torrent, flung itself hectically down the steep slope, snarling over the shallows, fighting savagely with the great boulders that opposed its way and furtively undercutting the banks of the gaunt primeval forest that stood impassively over it.

I called a halt in order to discuss our situation. If we continued much further, I feared that we might find ourselves in

A Papuan of Wetar standing by his out-rigger canoe.

a fairly serious predicament. "Not too late to abandon our project, and retrace our steps to the sea," I thought. I was still in the dark as to the location of the mysterious lake. To get any definite answer out of a Papuan concerning the distance to a given spot or the length of time it will take to arrive there, is out of the question. The answer is always evasive and simply concerns the speed of the walker, which is a relative thing. Being now nearly two days' journey from salt water and having only one day's supply of provisions, it would be an unnecessary risk and hardship to push ahead without definite assurance that we were within easy striking distance of our goal. The opportunity does not fall to everyone to do a little real exploring, and I was therefore all the more anxious to determine the nature of the mysterious lake that is lost in the wilderness of mountains on this Devil's Island. I knew that many abandoned Kampongs were to be found on its shores, so that it must be quite large.

The immediate problem was to determine in some way the distance that separated us from the hidden lake. So, scratching on the ground with my finger, I drew a map of the north coast of Wetar. Then I placed a pebble at the spot where Kampong Tara is situated, after which I made a zigzag mark indicating the course of the river Lihoetaoe. Then I took another pebble and, setting it down, explained that it represented the spot at which we were then sitting. A third pebble I juggled for a while in my hand tentatively, placing it here and there, and then saying, "Mana ayer besar?" (Where is the big water?) I handed the pebble to Maupelou. He caught on to the idea immediately. His face brightened and he took the pebble that I tendered him and threw it away. Then he got up and walked off several yards to a large boulder and, with the words, "gunung besar" (big mountain), he explained that it was necessary to climb the mountain and that the lake was down on the far

Dr. Dunn holding a python (Python timoriensis) *collected on Wetar.*

side. That finished me. According to his scale, we had not covered a third of the distance.

Terribly discouraged, I picked up my rifle and headed off on the back trail. The Malay coolies, delighted that the project had been abandoned, followed gleefully in my wake. I never found out how it was that Maupelou expected to reach the lake by noon of the first day, unless he thought me capable of white man's magic. So the big water, hidden away among the splintered mountains of Wetar, is still undisturbed, still waits for some more venturous white man to explore it.

While I had been gone, B. had had a novel experience. She had been up to one of the Papuan villages with Defosse.

"Upon our arriving at a group of huts that occupied a clearing in the jungle," she wrote, "there seemed to be a general meeting in progress. We waited, therefore, at the headman's house until the meeting should be over and he could speak to us. The usual silence prevailed, except for an occasional mutter and beating sound issuing from the place of meeting. Defosse said that he would go and take a look at the river nearby while I waited. As soon as he had gone with the gun, slinking figures sprang up from nowhere all around me, until there was a crowd pressing in closer and closer, without a sound. Of course, I could not speak a word to them, as only the headman speaks Malay, and I looked everywhere for him vainly. Finally, I jumped up, lit a cigarette with shaking fingers, and offered them around. These were clutched, examined and finally smoked. Just then, I saw the headman coming with a line of natives behind. I quickly pushed through to meet him, but he waved me off and passed on. Only then did I realize that he was draped in black, that there was a small coffin carried behind him, and that the mourners carried strange blocks of wood from which they seemed to read prayers and occasionally beat together. They quickly disappeared into the woods, all looking back at me. Of all times, we had chosen to come while a funeral was in progress! Not only that, but Defosse returned filled with consternation because he had disturbed the village maidens at their bath, and they had fled in terror to the forest. The only thing left for us to do was to flee in turn, but as we started to go, I grabbed Defosse, and said, 'For God's sake, run! Look at that leper coming towards us!'

"'Don't move,' he replied, and, to my horror, this grotesque creature came straight at me across the village square. I thus had plenty of time to notice his truly terrifying aspect- the long, greying hair on head and face, the wild eyes glaring from under beetling brows, and, worst of all, the twisted limbs covered with a single gaudy loin cloth. In his ears were huge silver rings, and from his mouth protruded the usual lump of betel nut. The juice of this nut drooled from his lips so that his beard and breast were stained as if in blood. His whole body looked as if hung in folds of mildewed shoe-leather, his skin being withered, and of a dead grey color. All he carried was the big knife which they usually wear in their sarongs, but in the determined way he came at me, I thought my time had come. Defosse whispered, 'Don't move, don't act afraid, and he will not hurt you.' So I stood my ground and waited. As he came nearer, one of our boys stepped between us to try to turn him, but with his eyes still fastened on mine, he brushed the boy aside and came on to within a few inches of my face. Then, with a quick thrust, he reached out and grabbed my hand in his shapeless one. After shaking it, he then shook hands with Defosse, and stood mouthing at us until some of his people took him away. He must be the village 'nut,' and Defosse thinks it is sun and old age, and not leprosy, that makes him look as he does. We washed thoroughly with disinfectant as soon as we got home, however."

Meanwhile, a varied assortment of pets had been accumulating in camp. Among them was the only deer on the island of Wetar, which we had brought with us on board. It would run up and down the beach with B. or wander around in the jungle near camp, looking very beautiful and wild. Occasionally it would cough at us in a strange, muddy voice, that reminded me of the crocodiles of Mr. Kipling. Then there was the turtle dove that hopped about with a broken wing. And there was the cuscus. The cuscus is a small marsupial, not unlike our own opossum, the first one, as it happens, of the Australian type that was ever observed by European eyes. It is arboreal, has a prehensile tail, and is nocturnal in its habits. Our specimen, a very small one, seemed rather to enjoy captivity. By night, she ambled along the outstretched limbs overhead, and by day she slept, rolled up cosily in a ball in her little basket, in which she appeared to be as comfortable as in the hollow tree to which she was accustomed. Whenever B. went to feed her, she unravelled herself, blinked in the sunshine, and then sat up on her hind legs. Holding a spoon in her little front paws, she would lick the contents dry. "Cuscusoo," as we called her, came to be a very precious member of the family, and eventually traveled all the way back to Java with us. She is now visiting the Captain in his Batavia home, and I feel sure that she is a most entertaining guest.

As time went on, the natives of Kampong Oohok deluged us with wild animals of every variety, including pythons, pit vipers, rat snakes, sea snakes, many different species of lizards, mice, about a dozen cuscus, civet cats, etc., etc. Many of these we took with us, and as several cockatoos, *Varanus*, lizards, and a runt pony from Sumbawa were already installed on board the boat, we had quite a long passenger list as we finally sailed away from Wetar.

On the return voyage we packed up our collections

The author's wife at the Raffles Hotel, Singapore, with her friend "John Bear".

preparatory to shipping them home. At Lomboc, Dr. Dunn was dropped off. He expected to collect for a week or ten days on Mt. Rinjani. Then we returned by rapid strides to Sourabaya, Batavia, and Singapore. Defosse sailed away for Saigon. He could hardly wait to return to his jungle and his impatience at the slightest delay destroyed what little pleasure the trip might have held for him. Lee Fai came down with a bad dose of malaria, and had to be taken to a hospital. One afternoon, B. went to see some wild animals that had recently been captured in Jehore. Here she found John Bear—John Bear of Malaya, and she brought him back, a wriggling black ball, to the Raffles Hotel, where he enjoyed complete liberty wandering from our room into the garden and back, as he pleased. John was a baby honey bear, *(Ursus malayanus)* about one month old. He was quite irresistible and eventually accompanied us all the way to New York.

Chu was the last one of our expedition to be disbanded. A more devoted and faithful servant could not be found. He came down to the boat with us—smuggled John Bear aboard—and arranged everything in our cabin in the most perfect order. Then he took his leave, for he was going back to his family in Peking. As he toddled down the gang plank, B.'s eyes filled. I felt a pain in my breast, as I realized that I might never see him again. Once, he turned smilingly and took off his hat and called back, "Gooby missy; gooby Masta." Then he waved a last farewell and the little figure disappeared from view. It may seem strange that one can develop such affection, that one can allow feeling to flow so deep for a Chinese "boy," but it is an experience common to travelers in the Orient. If only we could have brought him back with us! But there is always some law in this free country to prevent one from doing what one would like to do.

So the expedition was over, and we had a long weary road

to travel by way of Ceylon, Aden, Suez and Marseilles. In Paris, John Bear, who had entertained us hugely en route, went for a daily promenade in the Bois de Boulogne. No chain was needed. He followed us everywhere, ran around enjoying himself to his heart's content, always collecting a crowd of admirers.

On November 15th, we reached New York, where John Bear resided for three weeks in a kitchen before going out to winter in the country.

> "But the lizards, I'm sorry to say, (writes one of my friends)
> Became gaunt, and just faded away;
> For they only could thrive
> Eating chickens alive,
> Which was banned by the S.P.C.A."

The large Bima lizard, which after our departure from Sumbawa, was sent to the Amsterdam zoo, also died in captivity. Perhaps, however, it is just as well, for any reptile that has been caged is but a poor shadow of his former self. After watching these great carnivores in the wilderness of romantic Komodo, it was painful to see the broken-spirited beasts that barely had strength to drag themselves from one end of their cage to the other.

Surely, it is not all a matter of diet and a change of climate. Perhaps, as in the case of many mammals, *Varanus komodoensis*, in order to survive, demands the freedom of his rugged mountains.

CHAPTER IX

HERPETOLOGICAL
NOTES

THIS final chapter is along scientific lines, it consists almost entirely of quotations from Dr. Dunn's papers[1] published in the American Museum Novitates on the herpetological material collected by the expedition. It is divided into three sections. (1) Notes on *Varanus komodoensis*, (2) Lizards from the East Indies, (3) Snakes from the East Indies. The fourth section on the Amphibia is not yet completed.

"The notes hereinafter to be presented concerning the giant lizard of Komodo relate to the size attained; to the range; to its relationship to other living species; to its relationship to the various described *Varanid* fossils; and to the problem presented by the known facts.

"*Varanus komodoensis* was described by Ouwens in 1912. His material consisted of five specimens, all from Komodo. None of these were apparently sexed. The total length of these five was 2.9 m., 2.35 m., 2.2 m., 1 m., 1 m. The largest of these may be taken as the type of the species. It is at present mounted in the Museum at Buitenzorg.

[1] NOTES ON *VARANUS KOMODOENSIS*. CONTRIBUTIONS FROM THE DEPT. OF ZOÖLOGY, SMITH COLLEGE, NOS. 143, 144, 145. EMMETT R. DUNN.

164

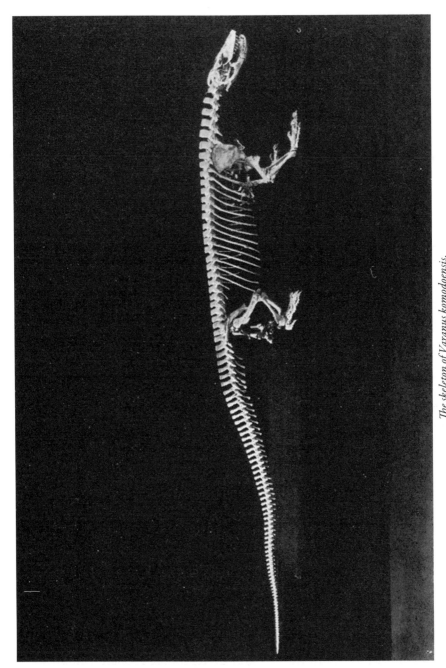

The skeleton of Varanus komodoensis.

Measurements: Total length, 9 ft 2 in.. Length of skull 1 ft.; body 3 ft. 8 in.; tail 4 ft. 6 in. Notice the sharp recurved teeth.

"De Rooij described a specimen, sex not mentioned, from Labuan Badjo on the west coast of Flores, in 1915. This specimen measured 2.66 m.

"The Duke of Mecklenburg in 1923 collected four specimens on Komodo. Of these three are in the Museum at Buitenzorg and were seen by me, while the fourth is in the Berlin Museum. None of these has the data concerning the sex. The three in Buitenzorg are under 2.5 m. The Berlin specimen, according to the authorities in Buitenzorg, is under 3m.

"Horst (1926) shot a specimen in Rinja which was just under 2 m.

"While a member of the Douglas Burden Expedition to the island of Komodo in 1926, I had the opportunity to take measurements and sex data on a number of individuals. I also saw a number whose lengths I am sure I did not underestimate. This material consisted of 17, whose sex I could determine, of ten additional which I could measure, of two skeletons found in an abandoned native trap whose lengths I could estimate, and of 27 specimens seen in the field by me personally which are additional to those already mentioned. I took considerable pains to count the actual number seen by me and to make this number an underestimate. In this way then I can assert that I saw on Komodo, in the flesh, at least, 54 specimens of *V. Komodoensis*. Of this 54 the largest measured 2765 mm. The second largest, not sexed, with broken tail measured head and body 1355 mm. The larger of the two skeletons had a lower jaw length of 250 mm. The two largest above mentioned had a lower jaw length of 255 mm. These were the four largest specimens to come under my observations.

"Of the seventeen specimens sexed, the fourteen largest were males. Of the three females the largest was 6 feet, 6 inches, or under 2 m. One more specimen has been sexed, the larger of two taken to Bima by natives and later sent to Holland. This was a male, the lower jaw measurement given by De Jong (1927) is 210 mm., thus indicating an animal distinctly smaller than either of the two larger ones mentioned above.

"Finally 20 skins were sent in the early days of 1927 by native poachers from Komodo to Macassar. Some of these skins found their way to London, where one came under the observation of Lord Rothschild (1927) and three of Mr. Burden. None of those seen were over 2.5 m.

"This evidence based on 73 specimens gives no indication that *Varanus komodoensis* reaches a length of over three meters. In fact the largest actual specimen on record is the type. It indicates that males alone reach great size.

"The only evidence of a greater size is contained in the original description among information transmitted to Ouwens by Mr. J. K. Van Steyn van Hensbroek. He says that Sergeant Beker shot one 4 m. long on Komodo, and that Messrs. Aldegon and Koch informed him that the former had shot some between six and seven meters in length on Komodo when they first visited the island. There is absolutely no material evidence to support these statements.

"The original description states that the animal is found on Komodo and on the west coast of Flores at Labuan Badjo. Horst (1926) mentions Mboera on the west coast of Flores and gives a definite record for Rinja, an island about the size of Komodo and between it and Flores. The only other island of any size nearby is Padar, between Komodo and Rinja. We saw tracks on the east coast of Padar, which were indistinguishable from those seen on Komodo, and the natives of Komodo told us that the lizards were found there. It is probable that these tracks were those of *komodoensis* and not *salvator* (the only other *Varanus* of the region) since apparently the two do not occur together, at least it is fairly certain that *salvator* does not occur on Komodo, although it is found on Sumbawa to the

west and on Flores to the east. Whether the two are found together in Flores, or what the relationship between them when,
or if, they meet is an interesting question. Horst (1926) says of
its range on Flores. That its range on Flores may have been for-
merly more extensive (than "a ... strikingly small region of the
extreme west") is very probable, although the animal is apparently restricted to a particular terrain, as may be deduced from
the regions in which it maintains itself at present. This type of
country consists of bare rocks and broken ground, grown up
with *alang-alang* grass and bushes mingled with open woods
and solitary *lontar* palms; although this country in the dry
season presents a very barren aspect it is not lacking in game.
Especially Komodo and Rinja ... are rich in game in the form
of deer and wild pig.' "

I agree with Dr. Dunn that *salvator* does not occur on
Komodo and that the tracks seen on Padar were undoubt-
edly those of *komodoensis*. It is not likely that two species of
Varanus lizards living in the same environmental niche should
occur together on the same range. Competition between the
two would exclude the weaker. Padar is a barren island consisting of uplifted coral. There is very little game and *komodoensis*,
therefore, digs for turtle eggs. I saw several places where they
had been at work on the beach and I also found the remains of
partially digested eggshells.

"The relationships of V. *komodoensis* to the living fauna
seem fairly simple. Using Boulenger's synopsis and characters
(scalation, shape and position of nostril and shape of tail) *komodoensis* comes nearest to *Varanus varius* of Australia. In scalation it differs form *varius* in having 80-97 ventrals as against
120-130 in *varius*; and in having much more enlarged nuchal
scales; the proportions are of course different, *varius* being a

much slimmer beast with a longer tail, and the coloration, especially of the throat and belly, is different, the black ventral bars, of *varius* being wholly absent.

"Near also are *giganteus, gouldii,* and *boulengeri* also all Australian species. But both *giganteus* and *gouldii* have more ventrals than *varius,* and neither have the large scales on the snout which are so prominent in both *varius* and *komodoensis.* Neither *gouldii* nor *boulengeri* have the terminal nostril which is present in the other three. I have not seen *boulengeri* but the other four all agree in the possession of osteoderms which are commonly supposed to be absent in *Varanidae.* These are present in the nuchal scales of both *varius* and *gouldii,* they seem to be all over *giganteus* and in *komodoensis* there is not only one below each scale, but on the head they form a curious network of anastomosing little bones, more like the skeleton of a star-fish than anything else. Perhaps other species of *Vararnus* might on examination belong with this group of species, although they form a section in Boulenger's key, but none I have seen do so. While *varius* and *komodoensis* are nearly allied, there is no possibility of performing a dichotomy on the genus since *Varanus* consists of a rather homogeneous series separated only by minor technical characters, and occasional more peculiar forms, each obviously related to another more normal. Thus *varius* could not be separated from the mass on any pretext, and there is no character whereby *komodoensis* could be removed without taking *varius* with it, save only proportions, where of more anon.

"Rothschild (1927) on the basis of one of the skins, makes the statement that *komodoensis* is allied to *albogularis* of West Africa, because the two have similar scales. I have not seen *albogularis,* but according to the literature the two differ in every other character, while as a matter of fact the scales of *komodoensis* and *varius* are exactly alike.

"The fossils allied to the living genus *Varanus* have been treated by Fejérváry (1918), by Gilmore (1922) and by Camp (1923).

"These authors allow at least three genera, *Varanus*, *Megalania*, and *Saniwa*. They furthermore allow the other two genera sub-family or family distinction form *Varanus*. Gilmore has found a sufficient difference between the skeleton of *Saniwa ensidens* and that of *Varanus salvator* to regard them as belonging to different genera of the same family. In this opinion I am content to follow him, seeing no reason for the erection by Camp of a subfamily *Saniwinae*.

"The Old World fossils are considered by Fejérváry. He himself had access to little of material, taking his information from descriptions and figures. I have access to none of it and am compelled to rely almost entirely on Fejérváry's paper. He regards the fossil material as representing two well established species from Europe, the earlier *cayluxi*, and the later *marathonensis*; one from India, *sivalensis*; and three from Australia, *priscus (Megalania)*, *dirus*, and *emeritus*. All the Australian fossils are late, probably Pleistocene. The Indian is Pliocene.

"The dates of the European ones are various, the later perhaps persisting until the Neolithic."

Then follows a detailed discussion of fossil *Varanids* which except for two paragraphs concerning the size of *Megalania*, i.e. *(Priscus)* which follow directly and general conclusions I will not include. One point however I would like to bring out, namely that *Varanus* appeared as a genus in Eocene times and that they are therefore, as a group, one of the oldest living lizards, dating back about sixty million years.

"Of the fossil species *sivalensis* has such different proportions from *komodoensis* that Lydekker's comparison with *salvator* and estimation of eleven feet may be accepted as the probable length. *Emeritus* seems to have been slim like *varius*. But half again as long. This might make a lizard ten to twelve feet in length. The maxilla referred to *dirus* is decidedly smaller than that of adult *komodoensis*, although the type tooth is larger. The maxilla is no longer than that of a six foot six inch *komodoensis* but teeth are about one third again as large, thus forming an intermediate in this respect between *komodoensis* and *priscus*, and leading one to suppose that *dirus* was not larger than *komodoensis*. A *komodoensis* maxilla the same length as that of *giganteus* has much larger teeth.

"On the basis of the vertebrae and assuming similar proportions *marathonensis* was two thirds the size of *komodoensis*. *Priscus* on the other hand was one third to two fifths larger, and on the basis of the ulna, the longest preserved limb bone of *priscus*, that animal would have been fourteen and a half feet long.

CONCLUSIONS

(1) "*Varanus komodoensis* is not known to reach a greater length than 3 meters.

(2) "Since only males are known to reach over two meters, the chances of a greater length than three meters being attained are small.

(3) "Of living species *Varanus varius* of Australia is the most similar.

(4) "Among the fossils, there is similarity in one or another character with *marathonensis*, *dirus*, *emeritus*, and *priscus* [i.e. *Megalania* which was considered to have attained a length of 30 ft.] Described and figured remains indicate that *komodoensis* is con-specific with none of these, and definite similarity in character other than that of weight of vertebrae is only indicated with the last three.

(5) "Of the fossils, the slimmer *sivalensis* and *emeritus* may have been ten to twelve feet in length. *Dirus* was probably smaller than *komodoensis*. *Marathonensis* was about six feet long. *Priscus* which, compared to *salvator*, has an estimated length of thirty feet, seems to have, when the more proper comparison to *komodoensis* is made, a length of not more than fifteen feet.

(6) "Since in regard to relative teeth size, *komodoensis* forms a transition between the normal *giganteus* and the large toothed *dirus* and *priscus*; and in regard to relative size of neural canal it and *marathonensis* form a transition between the normal type and the very heavy *priscus*, I am disinclined to regard *priscus* as having characters which necessitate generic and much less family distinction. Since the characters on which Camp considers *Sarniwa* as of a different subfamily are vertebral and are solely proportional, I prefer to consider it merely generically distinct from *Varanus* on the basis of the characters pointed out by Gilmore.

(7) "I regard the osseous development of *marathonensis, komodoensis*, and *priscus*, as extremely possible of independent origin. I therefore place no stress on a possible relationship to *marathonensis* where there are no other similar characters. This does not hold true for *priscus* or for *dirus*. I regard *komodoensis* as definitely an Australian type derived from an animal much like *varius* and intermediate between it and the two Australian fossil forms.

(8) "The significance of the preceding conclusions may be expressed as follows. From an ordinary *Varanoid* stock either larger and similar or larger and heavier forms may be produced under certain circumstances. These circumstances obtained in the Pleistocene in Australia. *Varanus komodoensis*, a modern offshoot from an Australian stock, now exists

in a certain restricted region in the Lesser Sunda Islands. The Australian element in this region seems to be a re-entrant from the Australian center of evolution (cf. *Cuscus*, a Diprotodont Marsupial, and hence probably a re-entrant, for if a relict from the movement of the early Marsupials into Australia were left in the Lesser Sundas, it would be one of the more primitive Polyprotodonts). Whether *komodoensis* arrived in its present state of development, or by what route it arrived at its present range, are two unanswerable questions. The picture of evolution which presents itself to my own mind is one of ordinary lizards, in arid country, and free from competition from the higher mammals (Australia in the pre-*Homo sapiens* pre-*Canis dingo* days), becoming large carnivores or perhaps carrion feeders. One of these, or one of the yet undifferentiated members of the same stock possessing the same potentialities of development, arrived by unknown means in the Lesser Sundas and met the vanguard of the Placentals. (Herbivores, as yet, and still unaccompanied by the higher and larger Carnivores, and as yet unfollowed by Man.) Here, these Australian emigrants persisted or developed, and here in the same, or in a latterly more restricted, range they can still be found."

In one point I disagree with Dr. Dunn. "The Australian element in the region," he says, "seems to be a re-entrant from the Australian center of evolution." The movement of early *Polyprotodont Marsupials* into Australia must have taken place before the origin of the Lesser Sunda Islands which occurred in the Pliocene. How, then, can there be any question of *Cuscus* being either a relict or re-entrant? Obviously the Diprotodont, along with the rest of the Lesser Sunda fauna, worked their way, bit by bit, from Australia on the one hand and Asia on the other into these Islands.

The question of the route by which *komodoensis* arrived from Australia is perhaps not as unanswerable as Dr. Dunn would have us believe. A glance at Brower's map of the Dutch East Indies reveals the Sahul Shelf extending northwestward from Australia nearly to Timor and northward to and including the Aru Islands and New Guinea.

The Sahul Shelf, like the Sunda Shelf, has in recent geological times, probably Pleistocene, been land. The jump from the northward limit of the Sahul Shelf to the Island of Timor is with the prevailing southeasterly trade winds, a fairly easy gulf to bridge when the various methods of accidental transportation are considered. From Timor, *komodoensis* could have made its way step by step along the old arc of volcanic islands to Sumba, just as *Salvator* has made its way similarly along the newer Lesser Sunda Island arc, from Java to Wetar. The next jump from Sumba to Komodo, under the influence of the same southeast trades, is no more difficult to bridge than the original Sahul Timor jump. Here at least is a tentative explanation.

A paper on the habits of *Varanus komodoensis* is being prepared by the author of this volume for the American Museum novitiates.

A detailed discussion of the importance of geological evidence in the matter of distribution of species in the East Indies will appear at a later date.

LIZARDS FROM THE EAST INDIES[2]

"The Lizards which form the subject of this paper were taken by the Douglas Burden Expedition to the Island of Komodo in the summer of 1926. They come from the islands of Pulo Weh (North of Sumatra), Java, Bali, Lombok,

---

[2]EMMETT REID DUNN. CONTRIBUTIONS FROM THE DEPT. OF ZOOLOGY, SMITH COLLEGE, NO. 145.

174

Dragon lizard group in the American Museum. A full grown male stands over a newly killed wild boar. A female is starting to tear the carcass to pieces. Another male (not seen in this photograph) advances upon them from the jungle on the left. Conflict is imminent.

Komodo, Padar, and Wetar, and number twenty-seven species and three subspecies, and 249 specimens. There are four new species and three new races in the collection. A number are, of course, new to the islands concerned, and these will hereinafter be designated as such.

"*Gymnodactylus defossei.* sp. nov.

Definition: A *Gymnodactylus* with no femoral or preanal pores; lateral fold of conical tubercles; dorsal tubercles very large; ventral scales small, 42 rows, smooth; tail with whorls of tubercles.

Type: A. M. N. H. No. 32108, Komodo at sea level. Paratypes, Komodo, 2000 ft., 11 (No. 32033-43).

Range: Komodo, from sea level to 2000 ft.

Description: Omitted.

Remarks: The type is the largest specimen and the only one taken in the low country. It was taken at night on June 19 on a tree close to the hut I shared with M. F. J. Defosse. He was with me when I secured it and I am associating his name with it. It was extremely common on the great rocks of the forest at 2000 feet altitude.

"Its relationships are somewhat to seek. The particular feature of this species are large tubercles on the dorsal region, and complete lack of femoral or preanal pores. These two characters are not found together in any of the species whose descriptions are accessible to me, and certainly in none from the East Indies. The large tubercles are found in *d'armandvillei* from Flores and in the new species from Wetar and possibly in

Dragon lizard group in the American Museum—A big male emerging from the jungle.

the oceanic *pelagicus*. Two, *Jellesmae* and *sermowaiensis* from Celebes and New Guinea respectively, lack pores, but neither have the enlarged regular tubercles. The Wetar form has pores.

"*Gymnodactylus Wetariensis* sp. nov.

Type: A. M. N. H. No. 32165 Paratypes No. 32160-4.

Type locality: Near Uhak, on the north coast of Wetar.

Range: Known only from the type locality.

Diagnosis: A *Gymnodactylus* with 12-13 femoral pores on each side; 11 preanal pores in an angular series; lateral fold of flat tubercles; dorsal tubercles very large; ventral scales in 38 rows; tail with whorls of tubercles.

Description: Omitted.

Remarks: These lizards, called, as was Gekko, '*ekke*' by the natives, were taken both at night and in the day time on trees. Their relationships are as far as the scalation is concerned with *d'armandvillei* of Flores and with *defossei* of Komodo. With regard to the femoral and preanal pores, *defossei* with none at all is quite different, while *d'armandvillei* with 18-19 femorals and no preanals is sufficiently distinct. Those having similar pores in the East Indies are *marmoratus* widely distributed with 12-13 preanals and 4-6 femorals; *baluensis* from Borneo with 9-10 preanals and 6-9 femorals and *mimikanus* from Papua with 7-14 preanals and 10-12 femorals. Of these *marmoratus* and *baluensis* have much smaller dorsal tubercles, but much the same coloration: *mimikanus* has a very different set of markings, and the tubercles, while in regular rows, are smaller.

Completed Komodo dragon lizard group.

"Hemidactylus frenatus Dumeril and Bibron.

8 specimens from: Komodo at sea level (No. 32105-7); Komodo at 2000 feet (No. 31995-6); Padar (No. 32018-9); Wetar (No. 32149). It was seen also in Lombok at Sembalun, and in Java at Buitenzorg. New to Komodo and to Padar.

"Cosymbotus platurus (Schneider).

One from Buitenzorg (No. 31988).

"Peropus mutilatus (Weigmann).

Two, from Komodo at 2000 feet (No. 31997), and from Wetar (No. 32150). New to both Islands.

"Gekko gecko (Linnaeus).

Ten, from: Komodo at sea level (No. 32109-10}; Komodo at 2000 ft. (No. 32048-9); and Wetar (No. 32226-31). It was also heard on Sangeang of the northwest point of Sumbawa, and at Buitenzorg. New to all three islands.

"Draco volans Linnaeus.

Three, from: Buitenzorg (No. 32020), and Bali (No. 32118-9).

"Draco reticulatus Gunther.

Two, from Komodo at sea level (No. 32094-5). New to the Islands.

"Draco timorensis Kuhl.

One, from Wetar (No. 32151). Native name 'Tokkai'

"*Aphaniotis acutirostris Modigliani.*

Three, from Pulo Weh (No. 32029-31)

"*Gonyocephalus chamaeleontinus* (Laurenti).

Five, from Tjibodas (No. 32024-8}. G. kuhli (Schlegel) is clearly a synonym.

"*Dendragama fruhstorferi* Boettger.

Three, from Tjibodas (No. 32021-3).

"*Varanus salvator.*

One from Bali. A specimen was seen at Suela, in Lombok. *Varanus komodoensis* Ouwens. This lizard was the main object of the expedition, and a discussion of its relationships has already been discussed. The number of specimens taken was limited by the Colonial Government, which in 1915 declared its range closed to hunting. Despite a certain amount of poaching in the early part of 1926, these lizards are fairly common on Komodo. We saw tracks on Padar, whence they had not been recorded. It is very decidedly an Australian type.

"*Mabuia multifasciata* (Kuhl).

Thirteen specimens, as fallows; Tjibodas (No. 31976, 32044-7), Bali (No. 32115-7), Sajong (No. 31999), Komodo at sea level (No. 32096), Komodo at 2000 Feet (No. 31991-3). Not hitherto known from Bali or Komodo.

"*Sphenomorphus florensis* (M. Weber)

Of this species I have seen the following specimens:
  Komodo, sea level 8 (No. 32097-104)

Komodo, 2000 feet, 21 (No. 32050-70)
Padar, 5 (No. 32000-4)
Flores, 1
Wetar, 18 (No. 32187-204)
Damma 1 (M. C. Z. No. 2099)

"These specimens are divisible into four local races on the basis of coloration. The single specimen from Flores is a young one and so like small specimens from Padar that I cannot separate the two. But all from Komodo can easily be told from those from Padar or Wetar. The Damma specimen is quite different. The species has not previously been recorded from Komodo or Padar. I find no differences in scalation. These races may be diagnosed as follows.

Sphenomorphus florensis nitidus ssp. nov.

Type: Amer. Mus. Nat. Hist. (No. 32068).

Paratypes 28 (No. 32097- 104, 32050-67, 32069-70).

Type locality: Komodo, 2000 feet alt.

Range : Komodo, sea level to 2000 feet.

Diagnosis: Young; brilliantly marked with a light and a dark dorso-lateral streak, extending on to the tail, and dark streak in front of groin; a very faint middorsal light streak; dorsal spotting very faint and irregular. Medium: dark dorsalateral stripe distinct only anteriorly; dorsal spots, nearly invisible. Adult: Almost without markings, top of head darker than sides with a dark line of demarcation; head not red; no black on throat; no post tympanic marking.

"*Sphenomorphus fiorensis ftorensis* (Weber).

Range: Padar and Flores.

Diagnosis: Young: A light dorso-lateral stripe, but dark dorso-lateral stripe indistinct and broken; no dark streak in front of groin; a prominent middorsal light stripe; dorsal spots large and distinct.

Medium: Dark dorso-lateral stripe broken; middorsal stripe prominent; dorsal spots large.

"Adult: almost without markings; top and sides of head same color no line of demarcation on sides of head; head with reddish tinge; throat flecked with black; no post tympanic mark. Remarks: Although amply distinct in both young and adult from the specimens of Komodo on the other sides of the narrow but deep and swift Linta Straits, I have been unable to find any characters to separate young from Padar from a young specimen from Flores, the type locality. I am, however, inclined to think that such characters exist, for de Rooij's description, presumably drawn from adults from Flores, does not agree very well with any adults I have seen from anywhere as in many other cases, more material is necessary before this problem can be settled.

"*Sphenomorphus ftorensis barbouri* sp. nov.

Type: Amer. Mus. Nat. Hist. No. 32203 Paratypes 17 No. 32187-202, 32204.

Type locality: North coast of Wetar, near Uhak. Range: Island of Wetar.

Diagnosis: Young: No light dorso-lateral line; dark dorso-lateral line only distinct anteriorly; no striping on tail; a marked middorsal light stripe; streak in front of groin very indistinct; small dorsal spots.

Medium: Much same as young; but dorso-lateral stripe fainter. Adult: dorsal-lateral stripe not apparent; middorsal stripe persistent; a light and a dark post tympanic streak; throat black. Remarks: Named in honor of Dr. Thomas Barbour, who lent me material of this species, and who was the first to recognize insular races of lizards in this region. The native name is "Tulupuhu."

"*Sphenomorphus florensis weberi* ssp. nov.

Type Mus. Comp. Zool. No. 2099, collected by the Siboga Expedition.

Type locality: Damma Island.

Range: known only from the type locality.

Diagnosis: Differs from all the preceding races in having no head markings, the belly and throat black, and in the dorsal region being dark with irregular light crossbars.
Remarks: Named in honor of Prof. Weber, who described the typical race.

"*Sphenomorphus striolatum* (M. Weber).

23 specimens from Komodo at 2000 feet elevation. Not seen in the lower country. Not previously known from Komodo.

"Sphenomorphus emigrans (van Lidth de Jeude).

Thirteen specimens from Wetar (No. 32205, 32207-18). May be referred to this species, already known from Pulo Sukar and Pulo Besar (both north off Flores), Sumba (everetti Boulenger), Samao near Timor, and New Guinea.

The specimens show great constancy in color, but much variation in scalation, and the generic and still more the specific assignment is rather a problem. The color is a light brown shading into white below. Both edges of all dorsal and lateral scales are dark brown. This is most regular dorsally, and gives the effect of longitudinal striping. In four the change in ground color is more abrupt, making the dark edges stand out almost as a lateral dark band. In three of these the edges of some of the dorsal scale rows are lighter than the others producing the effects of two narrow dorsal lines. In the largest (No. 32218) the animal is uniform brown above.

"Dasia smaragdinum elberti (Sternfeld).

Seven specimens from the north coast of Wetar (No. 32219-25). Scale rows 26-28. In color there was much variation; one was bright green on the sides as far as the groin, and above as far as the middle of the back, while the hinder part of the body was brown with black dots, another was similar, but the dots on the brown portion were a combination of black and white; two were brown with the black and white dots and a green tinge to the head and neck; two others were brown with spots all over and no trace of green. I saw no evidence that they changed color. This race has, as Sternfeld pointed out, the color of specimens from the Moluccas, but a higher scale count. He had only one specimen, collected by Elbert at Iliwaki on the south coast. This had 27 scale rows. Two of ours have 26; two 27, and three, 28.

The six I collected were all on tree trunks. The native name was "ular moin."

"Homolepida temmincki.

Twelve specimens from Tjibodas (No. 31979-90). No. 31981 has the prefrontals in contact, and 30 scale rows.

"Homolepida Schlegeli sp. nov.

Type: A. M. N. H. No. 31994, collected by E. R. Dunn, June 26 1926.

Type locality: Komodo. 2000 feet altitude.

Diagnosis: A Homolepida with 22 smooth scales, fourth toe longer than the third and with 10 subdigital lamellae; preanals enlarged.

Remarks: Only a single specimen of this species was taken. It was on the ground in the heavy forest, interspersed with great rock masses which forms the elevated center of Komodo. It is allied to *crassicauda* and *forbesi*, both of Papua. The former has more subdigital lamellae, and the latter more scale rows *H. temmincki* has been recorded from Samao in the Lesser Sundas, and I took it at Tjibodas in Java. It has many more scale rows, and the fourth toe is shorter, although it has the same number of lamellae. I thought it appropriate to associate the name of Schlegel with this species, since the name of Temminck is already associated with the Sundanese form.

"Leiolepisma fuscum (Dumeril and Eibron).

Twenty-one specimens form the north coast of Wetar (No.

32166-8) where the natives called them 'Diahna,' a name which also included the shortlegged *Sphenomorphus aruanus* and *undukitus*, and *Cryptoblepharus*. They had not previously been recorded from Wetar.

"Emoia similis, sp. nov.

Type A. M. N. H. No. 31977.

Type locality: Komodo, about 500-1500 feet altitude, Collected June 1926.

Diagnosis: An Emoia with short legs, barely meeting when appressed; interparietal fused; frontal longer than prefrontal; 22 lamellae under fourth toe; 28 smooth scales around body, allied to *cyanurm* and *kordoanum* but with shorter legs.

"These two lizards were taken on open grassy slopes, such as are found on Komodo from sea level to over 2000 feet. None were seen in the flat coastal grasslands, nor on the higher reaches of the hills. One was taken June 10 and another June 19. On the second occasion I climbed to about 1500 feet and the *Emoia* was taken "high up." These tiny lizards live in tall grass growing among loose stones, and are quite agile, so that the small number collected is no criterion of their rarity in their particular habitat.

Bornean specimens collected by H. C. Raven and kindly lent me by Dr. Stejneger are obviously *lessonii* (U. S. N. M. No. 51671, Borneo, 51691-7, 52976-83, Pulo Derawan, Borneo).

"Riopa bowringi (Gunther).

One specimen, No. 32032, from Pulo Weh. The scales are almost smooth. New to the Island.

"Cryptoblepharus boutonii furcata (M. Weber).

Eight specimens. No. 32152-9, from the north coast of Wetar. They have been compared with M.C.Z. No. 2094-5, from Larantaka, E. Flores, kindly lent me by Dr. Barbour and found to agree. Flores is the type locality for this form. The specimens were taken in the woods, either on the ground or climbing about in the trees. Five had 24, and three had 26 scale rows. New to the Island.

"Cryptoblepharus boutonii burdeni sp. nov.

Type Amer. Mus. Nat. Hist. No. 32006 Paratypes No. 32004-5, 32007.

Type locality: Padar, east coast.

Range: Known only from the type locality.

Diagnosis: Differs from the other races of *C. boutonii* in the higher number of scale rows (30-34), and in lacking any trace of light striping. The four median rows of dorsal scales are enlarged.

Habits: These lizards were discovered by Mr. Burden on rocks at the tide line on the east coast of Padar. Later I observed them there in great numbers, playing about on wet rocks. So numerous were they that when I had but one 22 shotshell left, I waited until three came close enough to each other and got them all with a single shot. On the wave cut bench of rock, beset with small pools, and alive with *Periopthalmus* and crabs, of various kinds, and wet by the waves of the rising tide these tiny lizards scuttled about unconcerned as to their larger neighbors. When I tried to catch some with my hands they ran into the water of the pools and two were caught there, clinging under water to the rocks.

"*Dibamus novae-guinae* (Dumeril and Bibron).

Twelve specimens from Uhak, on the north coast of Wetar, No. 32232-42. Not hitherto recorded from Wetar. The native name was "*tuhuopun.*"

Remarks: Disregarding races, there are now known from the Lesser Sunda thirty-two species of lizards. Of this number we met with twenty, a much larger proportion than the eight out of thirty-three snakes taken, which bears out the general experience of collectors as to the uncertainty of snake catching.

"Of the Lesser Sunda Lizards, twelve are apparently restricted to these islands. Of these the three species of *Gymnodactylus* offer no clue as to their provenance. Of the residuum two are western, two are likewise western in remote origin, but convey an impression of Muluccan or Celebesian affinities, while five are eastern.

"Of the non-restricted twenty, three are noncommittal, seven western, one Celebesian, and eight eastern.

"There is thus practically the same situation in lizards as in snakes with regard to the derivation of the endemics. With regard to the non-endemic lizards there are more eastern than western forms, while in the snakes there are more than four times as many westerners as Australians.

"Two factors seem to take part in producing this phenomenon, which is essentially that entrance into and survival in the Lesser Sundas has been relatively easier for eastern lizards than for eastern snakes. One factor is the greater relative migratory capacity of lizards (cf. the wide insular range of many forms, and the fact that from many islands lizards are known, but no snakes). The second is the climatic character of the Lesser Sundas, where the long severe dry season produces much open country and scanty forest. This condition is, I believe, more favorable for eastern than for western lizards. It is, also, more favorable for eastern than for western snakes, on the same line of reasoning, but eastern snakes, with their less capacity for extending their ranges, have not been able to take advantage of it. An example is *Calotes cristatellus*, which has gotten as far as Papua, but which is absent from the Lesser Sundas. Obviously, the explanation of its absence is not that it has been unable to reach these islands, but that the conditions are unsuited to it.

"At any rate, whatever the explanation, slightly over one fourth the lizard fauna has come from the west. About one fifth of these have been modified. Slightly under half have come from the east and over a third of these have changed. Thus, the relative proportion of endemics in the two faunal groups is about the same in the lizards as in the snakes, and indicates a more difficult route from the east, in both cases. There is, as in the snakes, a minute and largely modified old western element.

"In this group there is the largest element of unchanged eastern types in the herpetological fauna, but it does not exceed one fourth of the total. Even here, where the eastern element is most highly marked, the Lesser Sundas are faunally nearly as much Asiatic as Australian, while in the snakes and frogs the fauna is overwhelmingly Asiatic. In these groups, then, Wallace's Line is in no sense a faunal boundary.

"At least three of the eastern types reach Java, although the three next to appear are found in Komodo. Wetar, far to the east, and uncommonly isolated, has a fauna of fourteen lizards. Of these, five are western, five eastern, one of the middle fauna, and three noncommittal. One species and two races seem restricted to it. Remarkable on this isolated island are the number of burrowing forms, four lizards and a snake. Three are from the east, and two from the west, and they are the last animals one would expect to find there. The snake is peculiar to the island, but the lizards are widespread forms."

SNAKES FROM THE EAST INDIES[3]

"The snakes mentioned herein were taken by the Douglas Burden Expedition to the Island of Komodo in 1926. They come from the islands of Java, Bali, Lombok, Komodo and Wetar, and number twenty species, and sixty-six specimens. There are no new species or races, but there are seven new to Komodo, and five to Wetar, while Russell's viper, which was taken on Komodo, is new to the Lesser Sundas, and has for long been considered not to exist at all in the East Indies.

"*Typhlops braminus* (Daudin. Three, No.32112-4) from Bali. This very wide-spread form had not previously been taken on Bali.

"*Typhlops lineatus* (Boie). Four specimens from Buitenzorg, No. 31953-6.

"*Liasis mackloti* (Dumeril and Bibron). Two specimens from Uhak, on the north coast of Wetar, No. 32264-5. These make a new record for the island. They have a slightly greater number of scale rows (57-60) than the 49-55 given by De Rooij (1917) for specimens from Timor, Savu and Samao. Her largest specimen was 1680 mm. long, but one we had which disintegrated in transit, measured 2200 mm. The native name was 'sawa,' a name also used on Wetar for *Elaphe* and *Lycodon*.

---

[3] CONTRIBUTIONS FROM THE DEPARTMENT OF ZOÖLOGY, SMITH COLLEGE, NO. 144.

"Ptyas korros (Schlegel): A young specimen, No. 31948, from Buitenzorg. I am sure that a small specimen of this snake from the same locality served as the type of Barbour's *Liopeltis libertatis* (1910). The two descriptions are identical, and many points, especially the two loreals, in that of *L. libertatis* indicate a very different snake from the other *Liopeltis*. Miss Cochran and Dr. Stejneger have kindly examined for me the type in the National Museum and assure me that my opinion is correct.

"Liopeltis tricolor (Schlegel). One from Buitenzorg (No. 31951).

"Elaphe oxycephala (Boie). One from Buitenzorg, (No. 31946). This specimen has no loreal.

"Elaphe subradiata (Schlegel). Five, one from Komodo near the coast (No. 31973), and four from Uhak, on Wetar (No. 32251-4). New record for both islands. Another was seen on Komodo at 2000 feet half digested by a cobra which was a good deal smaller than the *Elaphe*. Both from Komodo had four dark lines anteriorly.

"Dendrophis formosus (Boie). One specimen from. Buitenzorg (No. 31947).

"Dendrophis pictus (Gmelin). Eight, from Buitenzorg (No. 31949), Suela on Lombok (No. 31934), Komodo near the coast (No. 31968), Komodo at 2000 feet (No. 31960), and Uhak on Wetar (No. 32247-50). It has not previously been recorded from Komodo or Wetar. The lateral stripe seems to die out gradually in the east. One of the Wetar specimens had eaten the only specimen of *Sphenomorphus aruanus* which we met with.

"Lycodon aulicus (Linne). Three from Komodo, near the coast (No. 31967), and from Uhak on Wetar (No. 32245-6). It reaches 2000 feet on Komodo for a piece of one was found in a cobra's stomach at that altitude. It had not been recorded from Komodo. The hemipenis of (No. 31967) is single, the sulcus is unforked, proximal half with hooks, distal with flounces. The Komodo specimen was climbing on a tree at night.

"Natrix chysarga (Schlegel). Three from Tjibodas in Java (No. 31939-40).

"Natrix subminiata (Schlegel). Two from Buitenzorg (No. 31950-1). In one of these on the left side only two labials enter the eye. In the other there are only seven labials, two entering the eye. Barbour (1912) has noticed this unusual variation in another Buitenzorg specimen.

"Calamaria linnaei (Boie). Two from Tjibodas, (No. 31944). In this species the hemipenis is calyculate and forked, and there is an apical awn.

"Psammodynastes pulverulentus (Boie). Nine from Tjibodas in Java (4500 ft.), (No. 31938), Sembalun (3500 ft.), (No. 31932-3, 31937), and Tanganea (5000 ft.), (No. 31935) on Lombok and Komodo at 2000 feet (No. 31936, 31961-3).

The Komodo examples seem slightly paler than do the Javanese. It has not yet been recorded from Komodo.

The hemipenis is forked and so is the sulcus, hooked throughout, on the distal half the hooks are in close set flounces.

"Homalopsis buccata (Linne). One specimen from Buitenzorg (No. 31945).

"Naja naia sputatrix (Boie). Five specimens from Komodo, three from sea-level (No. 31957-9), and two from 2000 feet (No. 31974-5). At least two others were seen. One had eaten a *Lycodon aulicus*, and one an *Elaphe subradiata*. They have feebly developed hoods which they seldom spread.

"I use the Javanese racial name for this easternmost cobra, already recorded from Lombok, Sumbawa, Flores and Alor. Not hitherto taken on Komodo.

"Latimuda colubrina (Schneider). One specimen from Uhak on Wetar (No. 32244) not hitherto recorded from the coast of this island.

"Vipera russelli (Shaw). Two from Komodo (No. 31971-2). Not hitherto recorded from this island. These two specimens of Russell's viper have been carefully compared with specimens from India kindly loaned me by Dr. Barbour and found not to differ. They have 29 scale rows, and 154 ventrals. Both Dumeril and Bibron (1854) and Boulenger (1896) have recorded each, a single specimen from Java. Ditmars mentions some from Sumatra collected by Mr. Rudolf Weber. The snake is not known from the Malay Peninsula and no recent specimens are known from Java, so that De Rooij was inclined to doubt the earlier records. Now, however, they appear more plausible, although it is very remarkable to find a true viper so far east. They were taken in the lower hills of the island.

"Trimeresurus gramineus fasciatus Boulenger (?). Specimens from Komodo (sea-level No. 31969- 70), (2000 feet No. 31964-6) and Uhak on Wetar (32257-61). They were very common at Uhak and several more were seen. One of those taken at sea level on Komodo had eaten a mouse, and two from 2000 feet had eaten *Kaloula pulchra*.

"It had not previously been recorded from Komodo or Wetar.

"Further characters of this race are that all from Komodo and Wetar have 21 scale rows and the supranasals in contact.

"The native name on Wetar was '*oily*.'

Remarks: Of the eight species of terrestrial snakes taken in the course of the expedition on the islands east of Wallace's Line seven show Asiatic affinities and one (*Liasis mackloti*) Australian. Of the seven Asiatics one (*Elaphe subradiata*) is not known from west of Wallace's Line, and this form is so like *Elaphe enganensis* of Engano Island, south of Sumatra, that it appears less like an endemic Lesser Sunda form than a relict form of an earlier fauna, now lingering in two very slightly differentiated species in the Lesser Sundas and in Engano. The *Liasis*, found on Wetar, for the first time, was already known from Savu, Samao, and Timar, and is very slightly different from Australian and Papuan species. The headquarters of the genus is eastwards, however, and marks as clearly an Australian element in the snake fauna of Wetar as the species of *Lycodon*, *Dendrophis*, *Elaphe* and *Lachesis* on the same easternmost island of the chain indicate an even stronger Asiatic element. The one Australian type found is distinct, as is only one out of seven of the Asiatics.

"Of the thirty-three terrestrial snake species known from the Lesser Sundas, ten are restricted to these islands. Of these ten, *Liasis mackloti*, *Python timoriensis*, *Typhlops elberti*, and *Typhlops florensis* may well be eastern. Three have definite western affinities and three, while as definitely western in their affinities, have more alliance with an endemic or an earlier fauna which may be found in the Moluccas or in Celebes. This last element does not necessarily mean migration to or from these regions to the Lesser Sundas. More probably this series of forms passed out from Asia along a northern and a southern route. Whatever may have been the means of migration, it has been much easier for snakes to get from Asia to Wetar, more than a thousand miles of sea and islands, than from Cuba to Haiti over a strait of fifty miles. Four snakes are known in common from the first two (out of seven species known from Wetar), while only one species of snake is common to Cuba and Haiti, although each island has about twelve species.

"Of the forms not restricted to the Lesser Sundas, four seem definitely eastern, one Moluccan, and eighteen western.

"Thus there is a great difference in the quality of the emigration. Over half the snake fauna has come over unchanged from the west, and only three of this group have changed.

"Of the nine easterners, four have undergone modification. The slight trace of an endemic or a Moluccan element consists of three species restricted to the region, and one more wide ranging (*Brachyorrhus albus*) and all are definitely western in their larger affinities.

"This seems to indicate an overwhelming modern unmodified Asiatic element, a small and rather modified Australian element, and a minute and modified old Asiatic element. For Mammals of course this situation is well known to exist in the East Indies, with the old Asiatic element best marked in Celebes.

"The eastern element is naturally strongest in the more eastern islands, although of the species considered eastern, one occurs on Lombok, and two on Flores. The snakes of the easternmost isolated island of Wetar are six out of seven western types, and only one of them is modified (*Cylindrophis boulengeri*).

"The difference in island speciation to be found in the same group in the East Indies and in the West, has, of course, nothing to do with the provenance of the fauna. The chief difference between the islands on which these phenomena are most marked is that the Greater Antilles are non-volcanic, while the Sundas are noted for the number and activity of their volcanoes. The correlation is sufficiently obvious. It would seem that migration from island to island is easier when these islands are volcanic in nature."

LITERATURE CITED.

1889 De Vis, on Megalania and its Allies, Proc. Roy. Soc. Queensland, VI., p. 98, pl. IV.

1912 Ouwens. On a large *Varanus* Species from the Island of Komodo, Bull. Jardin Botan. Buitenzorg (2) VI. p. 1, pl. 1-3.

1915 De Rooij. The reptiles of the Indo-Australian Archipelago, I, p. 150, f. 64.

1918 Fejérváry. Contributions to a Monography on Fossil Varanidae and on Megalanidae. Ann. Mus. Nat. Hungarici 16, p. 341.

1919 Schmidt. Contributions to the Herpetology of the Belgian Congo, I, Bull. Amer. Mus. Nat. His. 39, L. 8-10.

1922 Gilmore. A New description of Saniwa ensidens Lendy, an extinct Varanoid Lizard from Wyoming. Proc. U.S. Nat. Mus. 60, p. 1. pl. 1-3.

1923 Camp. Classification of the Lizards. Bull. Amer. Mus. Nat. Hist. 48, p. 289.

1926 Horst. *Varanus Komodoensis*. Tropische Natuur. 15, pp. 118-121.

1927 Rothschild. Note on Veranus *komodoensis*. Proc. Zool. Soc., London, p. 283.

1927 De Jong. Anatomische Notizen über *Varanus komodoensis*, Ouwens. Zool. Anz. 70, p. 65.

NOTE: The snaring of the large lizard which eventually escaped was actually not witnessed by any white man. The account as given in Chapter VII has been drawn from similar scenes that were witnessed.

CHECK OUT ALL THE
B&C CLASSIC BOOKS

—

AFRICAN GAME TRAILS

RANCH LIFE AND THE HUNTING TRAIL

By Theodore Roosevelt

—

A HUNTER'S WANDERINGS IN AFRICA

RECENT HUNTING TRIPS IN
NORTH AMERICA

By Frederick Courteney Selous

—

CAMP-FIRES IN THE CANADIAN ROCKIES

CAMP-FIRES IN DESERT AND LAVA

By William T. Hornaday

—

DRAGON LIZARDS OF KOMODO

By W. Douglas Burden

—

WILDERNESS OF THE UPPER YUKON

By Charles Sheldon

—

Visit www.boone-crockett.org